WOMEN IN MUSLIM FAMILY LAW

Contemporary Issues in the Middle East

WOMEN IN MUSLIM FAMILY LAW

John L. Esposito

Syracuse University Press

First Paperback Edition 1982
        98 99   6 5 4 3

Library of Congress Cataloging-in-Publication Data

Esposito, John L.
  Women in Muslim family law.

  (Contemporary issues in the Middle East)
  Includes index.
  1. Women—Legal status, laws, etc. (Islamic law)
I. Title. II. Series.
LAW   346.5601'34   81-18273
ISBN 0-8156-2256-2   345.606134   AACR2
ISBN 0-8156-2278-3 (pbk.)

Manufactured in the United States of America

For Jean and my parents, who are always there.

JOHN L. ESPOSITO is Loyola Professor of Middle East Studies, College of the Holy Cross. He has served recently as President of the Middle East Studies Association of North America and is Editor-in-Chief of the *Encyclopedia of the Modern Islamic World.* Among his publications are: *Islam: The Straight Path, The Iranian Revolution: Its Global Impact, Islam in Asia: Religion, Politics, and Society, Islam and Politics, Islamic Threat: Myth or Reality,* and *Voices of Resurgent Islam.*

CONTENTS

PREFACE

A RAB OIL AND THE SPECTER OF THE ISLAMIC RE-SURGENCE during the 1970s have focused attention on the Muslim world in a way unparalleled in modern times. The Islamic revival occurring in most Muslim countries has manifested itself at both the personal and political levels. Along with increased mosque attendance, concern for more Islamic forms of dress, and a proliferation of religious literature, Islam has also re-emerged in Muslim politics. Islam is used by governments to legitimate their rule and policies, and it also serves as an umbrella for opposition forces who seek to topple "un-Islamic governments." While Iran has received the greatest media attention, variations on this theme may be found in Pakistan, Saudi Arabia, Egypt, Syria, and Malaysia.

Although profound differences between one Muslim country and another exist, common factors in the Islamic revival include a growing disillusionment with the West, a tendency to blame westernization and secularization for the social disruption and moral decline that has accompanied modernization, and the desire to provide more cultural continuity between modernity and tradition. While past sociopolitical change is seen as a process of critical imitation of the West, the call today is for modernization which is more self-consciously rooted in Islamic history, beliefs, and values. This concern to follow a path of cultural adaptation, rather than to displace the old through a wholesale adoption of the new, raises the practical questions: Does Islam (the Islamic tradition) possess the resources to support and sustain reinterpretation and reform, and thus respond effectively to the demands of modernity? Is Islamic reform possible? What does this mean for women and the family?

Muslim family law provides the primary example of Islamic reform in the twentieth century. Islamic law (the Shariah) constitutes the ideal blueprint for Muslim society. It is a divinely revealed law, a comprehensive legal system whose laws govern duties to God (*ibadat*, ritual observances such as prayer, almsgiving, fasting) and duties to one's fellow man (*muamalat*, social transactions which include commercial, penal, and family laws).

Reflecting the centrality of the family in Islam, family law has been the heart of the Shariah and the major area of Islamic law that has remained in force to govern the lives of more than 800 million Muslims from North Africa to Southeast Asia. While most areas of Islamic law have been replaced by modern western legal codes, Muslim family law has provided the major area of Islamic reform.

Change in family law, then, is significant both as an index of social change and as an illustration of Islamic reform, its methodology, and problems. Traditionally, the primary role of the Muslim woman has been that of wife and mother, living within the extended family in a patriarchal society. Islamic laws set the standards regarding women's rights and duties; modern reforms have been advocated as seeking to protect and improve women's status and rights in a changing society with its movement from the extended family to a more nuclear family. Therefore, among the fundamental questions which Muslims face are: Can Islam change? Can change embody an Islamic rationale that reflects continuity between an Islamic past and modern reforms?

Although studies of family law reform exist, they do not provide the background (development of traditional family law) and context (traditional status of women and the family) necessary for understanding the significance of modern reforms. Secondly, western scholarship has generally approached the subject from without rather than from within, exploring the resources of the Islamic tradition to supply a rationale and systematic methodology for Islamic reform. This study will first discuss the historical and legal context for reform (the origins, development, and content of Islamic law).

It will then analyze the process, methodology, and extent of modern legal reforms, focusing on changes in Egypt and Pakistan, countries which lend themselves to comparison and contrast. Both countries officially follow the same traditional school of Islamic law (Hanafi), and both were initiators of family law reform. Moreover, in both Egypt and Pakistan, strong movements to establish more Islamically-oriented societies have surfaced. The introduction of more Islamic law has become an important issue in Egyptian and Pakistani politics. A major aspect of this effort to establish an Islamic identity more firmly has been a re-examination of the question: What does it mean to be a Muslim woman? This is reflected in women's return to more traditional Islamic forms of dress and behavior, as well as calls for the repeal of certain aspects of family law reform which are seen as un-Islamic. However, significant differences between the Egyptian and Pakistani experiences exist, both in the extent of reform and the legal methodology utilized.

Reform efforts in each country exemplify and illustrate the major legal approaches employed thus far in the Muslim world, as well as the problems and issues surrounding Islamic reform. Where relevant, major family law reforms from other parts of the Muslim world will also be discussed to provide a total picture of the changing status of Muslim women and the possibilities for legal reform. Finally, this study will delineate those dynamic resources in the Islamic tradition which can provide a methodology for future reforms that responds to the continued and changing needs of Muslim society.

While this study is inescapably technical in nature, it has been organized and written to accommodate the nonspecialists as well as the specialists. Diacritical marks have been omitted to simplify reading and to reduce production costs. A brief bibliography has been included for further reading.

I am indebted to Ismail R. al-Faruqi (Temple University) and Hassan Hanafi (Cairo University) for my early training in Islamic Studies and for their many helpful comments and observations throughout the years. Several typists—Barbara Letourneau, Lorna Mattus, Elizabeth Stebbins and Kathleen Lauring—have worked on successive versions of this manuscript. Finally, my wife Jean, my parents, and brothers have been and continue to be an inestimable source of inspiration and support.

Worcester, Massachusetts   JLE
Summer 1981

WOMEN IN MUSLIM FAMILY LAW

1

The SOURCES OF ISLAMIC LAW

HE CENTRAL FACT OF THE MUSLIM RELIGIOUS EXPERI-
ENCE IS ALLAH (GOD). In contrast to the polytheism of
pre-Islamic Arabia, the God of the *Quran* is one and transcendent:
"And your God is One God: there is no God but He, Most
Gracious, Most Merciful" (II:163). This God, the creator and
sustainer of the universe, is the overwhelming concern of the
believer.[1] Man's duty is obedience and submission *(islam)* to the
will of God. The submission incumbent upon the Muslim, however, is not that of mere passivity; rather, it is submission to the
Divine imperative, to actively realize God's will in history. Thus,
the *Quran* declares that man is God's vicegerent on earth (II:30;
XXXV:39). God has given him the Divine Trust *(amanah)*
(XXXIII:72; VI:165), and it is on the basis of how man executes his
vicegerency that he is to be either rewarded or punished (VI:165).

Man's obligation to realize the divine imperative in space
and time is communal as well as individual. The Islamic community *(ummah)* is to be the dynamic vehicle for the realization of the
divine pattern (III:110; II:148; LVIII:109; CIII:2–3), and, as such,
the *ummah* is to serve as an example to other peoples of the world
(II:143; VI:72; X:45–46).

1

The Muslim concern not simply to know the divine will but also to execute it, inspired the early Muslim community's expansion and conquest of Arabia, the Eastern Byzantine Empire in Palestine, Syria, Lebanon, the Persian (Sasanid) Empire in Iran and Iraq, and Egypt. However, the realization of the Muslims' religious vision to transform the world was not a simple task. The geographical expansion of Islam resulted in many new problems which raised the question, "How is the divine will to be realized in this situation?" Since the *Quran* is not a law book, i.e., not a collection of prescriptions providing a legal system, and because the Prophet was no longer alive to resolve problems, the early Caliphs, and later, during the Umayyad period (661–750), the judges *(qadis)* shouldered the responsibility of rendering legal decisions.

In the eighth century, due to a growing dissatisfaction with Umayyad rule and a belief that its courts had failed to incorporate and implement the spirit of *Quranic* reforms, early schools of law *(madhhab,* pl. *madhabib)* emerged in major cities of the empire. These schools originally consisted of pious Muslims in Mecca, Medina, Kufa, and Baghdad. In time, they attracted followers who associated themselves with one of these great early leaders *(Imams)*—men like Abu Hanifa (d. 767), Malik ibn Anas (d. 796), Muhammad al-Shafii (d. 820), and Ahmad ibn Hanbal (d. 855). In this sense, they came to be viewed respectively as the founders of the Hanafi, Maliki, Shafii, and Hanbali schools. While there were originally many schools of law, only these four survived the test of time.[2] Because of the breadth of the *ummah* and the varying cultural situations and practices which it embraced as well as the number of law schools, many differences existed both in the legal techniques employed and the substantive law developed. Muhammad ibn Idris al-Shafii (d. 204/819), the father of Muslim jurisprudence, sought to systematize the methodology of the law schools and thus limit the growing diversity in Islamic law. Shafii came at a critical time in Muslim history. His actions brought about the culmination of long-term conflicts between two schools of legal thought. The first relied on the free use of reasoned opinions (the *ahl al-ray)* of the ancient schools, while the second, the traditionist *(ahl al-hadith),* relied upon the *Quran* and the *Sunnah* of the Prophet as the only valid sources of legal doctrine. This second, traditionist movement criticized the *ahl al-ray* schools for their dependence on the practice of their own school and for their free exercise of personal opinion *(ray)* because it produced too much diversity of doctrine. To meet the need for a more systematic legal method, Shafii, who deplored the great variety of doctrine, sought to limit the four sources of law *(usul al-fiqh)*, and thus establish a common methodology for all schools of law. As a result of his efforts, by the ninth century, classical theory of law fixed the sources of Islamic law at four: the *Quran, Sunnah* of the Prophet, *qiyas* (analogical reasoning), and *ijma* (consensus).

THE SOURCES OF ISLAMIC LAW

The *Quran*

The *Quran* is the revelation of God, the central fact of the Islamic religious experience. As the very word of God, for Muslims the *Quran* is the presence of the numinous in history (space and time).

Quranic revelation is not that of the transcendent God, but rather of his Divine Will which man is to follow: "Here is a plain statement to men, a guidance and instruction to those who fear God" (III:138). Thus, the primary material source of the revealed law is quite naturally the *Holy Quran*, the sourcebook of Islamic values. While the *Quran* does contain prescriptions about matters that would rank as legal in the strict, narrow sense of the term, these injunctions, in fact, comprise but eighty verses. The bulk of *Quranic* matter consists mainly of broad, general moral directives as to what the aims and aspirations of Muslims should be, the "ought" of the Islamic religious ethic.

The *Quran* was revealed to Muhammad over a period of twenty-three years in order to meet the needs of the Islamic society in Mecca and then in Medina. It gradually provided an Islamic ideology for the community and, in the process, modified or supplemented existing customs not meeting Islamic standards.

Those verses most important for the development of legal doctrine came about in Medina during the growth of the community-state. Verses were revealed which replaced or revised old tribal customs with new rules. The gradual replacement of existing customs that did not meet Islamic standards is well illustrated by the *Quranic* prohibitions of liquor and games of chance. In the early years the use of alcohol and gambling had not been prohibited and hence, the old custom continued to be followed. The first prescription against the old custom is given in the form of advice: "They ask thee concerning wine and gambling. Say: In them is great sin and some profit, for man; but the sin is greater than the profit" (II:219). Later, Muslims were prohibited from offering prayers in drunkenness: "O ye who believe! Approach not prayers with a mind befogged, until ye can understand all that ye say" (IV:43). Later still, liquor and gambling were fully prohibited with the explanation: "Satan's plan is [but] to excite enmity and hatred between you with intoxicants and gambling, and hinder you from the remembrance of God and from prayer: Will ye not then abstain?" (V:94).

Some of the most important and fundamental reforms of customary law were made by the *Quran* in order to improve the status of women and strengthen the family in Muslim society. Three main areas of *Quranic* reform were marriage, divorce, and inheritance. In the realm of marriage, for example, the *Quran* commands that only the wife and not her father or other male relatives should receive the dower *(mahr)* from her husband: "And give the women [on marriage] their dower as a free gift" (IV:4). Thus, the woman becomes a legal partner to the marriage contract rather than an object for sale. In addition, unlimited polygamy was curtailed and the number of wives limited to four. However, a final injunction stressed that if the husband did not believe that he could be equally fair to each of his wives, he should marry only one: "Marry women of your choice, two, three or four. But if ye fear that ye shall not be able to deal justly [with them] then only one" (IV:3). And, in another place, the *Quran* continues: "Ye are never able to be fair and just as between women, even if that were your ardent desire" (IV:129).

In the area of divorce, in order to provide an opportunity for reconciliation, an important *Quranic* reform calls for a waiting period *(iddah)* of three months, or, if a wife is pregnant, until delivery of her child, before her husband can divorce her: "Such of your women as have passed the age of monthly courses, for them the prescribed period, if ye have any doubts, is three months, and for those who have no courses [it is the same]: For those who carry [life within their wombs], their period is until they deliver their burdens" (LXV:4).

Inheritance provides another example of *Quranic* reform of existing practice. The advent of Islam brought a shift from tribal allegiance to the solidarity of the Islamic community *(ummah)*, a brotherhood of believers which was to transcend all tribal and racial loyalties. Coupled with this reform was a concern for the strength of the family and the members within it, especially women. These concerns are exemplified in the *Quranic* regulations governing inheritance. Succession in tribal customary law had been solely based on an (male) agnatic system *(asaba* i.e. kinship and thus inheritance through male descent). The *Quran* modified this system by introducing the golden rule of inheritance, the primacy of distribution of certain fixed shares to several categories of Quranically designated heirs comprised mainly of the nearest female relatives excluded under the agnatic system. After these *Quranic* claims have been satisfied, the residue of the estate is awarded to the nearest male (agnate) relatives.

The *Sunnah* of the Prophet

Quranic values were concretized and interpreted by the second material source of law, the *Sunnah* of the Prophet. Just as during the lifetime of the Prophet, Muslims turned to him for decisions, so after his death, they looked to the Prophetic example for guidance. In classical theory, *Sunnah* of the Prophet consists quite simply in the normative model behavior of the Prophet. The importance of the *Sunnah* of the Prophet is rooted in the *Quranic* command to obey and follow Muhammad: "O ye who believe, obey God and obey the Apostle... if ye differ in anything, refer it to God and His Apostle" (IV:59), and again, "Ye have indeed in the Apostle of God a beautiful pattern of conduct for any one whose hope is in God and the Final Day" (XXXIII:21).

Technically, *Sunnah* is divided into three categories: (1) *al-sunnah al-qawliyah*, the Prophet's statements and sayings; (2) *al-sunnah al-filiyah*, his deeds; and (3) *al-sunnah al-taqririyah*, his silent or tacit approval of certain deeds which he had knowledge of.

The record of the Prophetic words and deeds is to be found in the narrative reports or traditions *(hadith)* transmitted and finally collected and recorded in compendia. The authoritative collections of *hadith* were not compiled until the middle of the ninth century, by which time a great mass of diverse *hadiths* reflected the variety of legal opinion developed over the past two centuries of juristic reasoning in the legal schools. Recognition that the *hadith* literature included many fabrications led to a concerted effort to distinguish more clearly authentic traditions. These *hadiths* were evaluated through a painstaking attempt which produced the new Muslim science of *hadith* criticism *(mustalah al-hadith)*.

Criteria were established for judging the trustworthiness of narrators. For example, they had to be adult Muslims, legally responsible, of good moral reputation (rational, just, moral) and known to have good memories. Then a link *(sanad)* by link examination of the transmissional chain was made to trace the continuity of the tradition back to the Prophet.

On the basis of this examination of the chain of narrators, *hadiths* were generally classified from the point of view of narration as *mutawatir* (continuous), *mashhur* (well-known), and *ahad* (isolated). *Mutawatir* refers to a tradition whose chain of narrators *(isnad)* is consistent and continuous. *Mashhur* (well-known) refers to those traditions which were widely disseminated and whose narration could be traced back to one or two narrators in the time of the Prophet. *Ahad* (isolated) referred to traditions whose last link *(sanad)* in the chain of narrators was limited to one authority. This last category was inferior to the first two and was thus considered weaker. These categories were divided into subcategories to further distinguish the strength or weakness of traditions.

The second criteria for judging the *hadith*, an examination of its matter or *matn*, was used by asking if this matter contradicted the *Quran*, a verified tradition, reason, or the consensus of the community. After the traditions had been subjected to both external (narrators) and internal (subject matter) examination, they were labeled according to the degree of their strength or authenticity as *sahih* (authentic), *hasan* (good) and *daif* (weak). Of the six major collections of *hadith* of the Prophet, the *Sahihs* of al-Bukhari (d. 870) and that of Muslim (d. 875) have enjoyed an especially high reputation. However, as shall be discussed in Chapter IV, questions regarding the authenticity of the *hadith* remained.

Qiyas

Muslims' concern to be true to the material sources (*Quran* and *Sunnah* of the Prophet) of their faith led to the development of *qiyas* (analogical reasoning). *Qiyas*, the third source of law, is a restricted form of *ijtihad* (personal reasoning or interpretation); it is reasoning by analogy. The noted jurist Shihab al-Din al-Qarafi (d. 1285) defined it as "establishing the relevance of a ruling in one case to another case because of a similarity in the attribute (reason or cause) upon which the ruling was based."[3]

The key to the use of *qiyas* is the discovery of the *illa* (reason or effective cause) for a *Shariah* rule. If a similar *illa* was judged to be present in the new case under consideration, then the *Shariah* judgement was applied. Among the earliest usages of *qiyas* was the fixing of the minimum dower *(mahr)*. An analogous situation was established between the loss of virginity due to marriage and the *Quranic* penalty for theft — amputation of the hand. The sums of the minimum dower in Kufa and in Medina were equivalent to the established values which stolen goods had to reach in Kufan and Medinan teaching, respectively, before amputation was applicable.[4]

Ijma

The fourth source of law, *ijma*, has played a key role in the development of Islamic law. The classical and standard definition of *ijma* is the unanimous agreement of the jurists of a particular age on a specific issue. *Ijma* derived its authority as a source of law from the *hadith* that records the Prophet as saying, "My Community will never agree on an error."

In the early community, however, *ijma* was not a formalized practice. It developed after the death of Muhammad and the consequent loss of his guidance in legislative matters. *Ijma* began as a natural process for solving problems and making decisions, depending upon the approval of majority opinion to insure against individual fallible reasoning *(ijtihad)*.

Two kinds of *ijma* should be distinguished. The *ijma al-ummah* refers to the consensus of the whole community. It is used in matters of religious practice, as for example, the ritual of pilgrimage to Mecca that is practiced by all pilgrims. However, authority for this *ijma* is not found in early legal texts. The second type, *ijma al-a immah*, meets with the classical definition, the consensus of religious authorities regarding interpretation of a *Quranic* text or tradition, or a development of legal principle.

Ijma contributed significantly to the corpus of law *(fiqh)*. If questions arose about a *Quranic* text or tradition, or a problem for which no *sunnah* (practice) of the community existed, the jurists applied their own reasoning *(ijtihad)* to arrive at an interpretation. Over a period of time (perhaps several generations), one interpretation would be accepted by more and more doctors of law. Looking back in time at the evolved consensus of the scholars, it could be concluded that an *ijma* of scholars had been reached on this issue.

The general consensus of Muslim jurists *(faqih,* pl. *fuqaha)* has always been that the *Shariah* is concerned with human welfare and based upon justice and equity. Three of the four Sunni schools of law developed and utilized the following subsidiary legal methods whose primary purpose was the guaranteeing of justice and equity: *istihsan* (juristic preference), *istislah* (public interest), and *istishab* (presumption of continuity). All are considered forms of *ijtihad.*

Istihsan

Istihsan, juristic preference, is a principle associated with the Hanafi school. Where strict analogical reasoning led to an unnecessarily harsh or rigid result, juristic preference was exercised to achieve equity. Proponents of this principle could cite the *Quran* to support their position: "Those who listen to the Word and follow the best *(ahsanahu)* meaning in it: Those are the ones whom God has guided and those are the ones endowed with understanding." (XXXIX:18; XXXIX:55).

Istislah

The second supplementary principle of law is *istislah*, a concept associated primarily with the Maliki school which accepted public interest or human welfare *(maslaha)* as a source of law. *Al-masalih al-mursalah* denotes public interests which are not covered by any *Shariah* text and are thus not textually specified *(mursal)*. The method of *istislah* consists in the determination by the jurist of man's best interest in a case and the rendering of a judgement that will promote it. *Istislah* is a juristic method, a tool of interpretation and not a material source of substantive law. It is based on the belief that God's purpose in the *Shariah* is the promotion of human welfare.

Istislah was not simply utilitarian; it did not develop as a freewheeling principle, but rather as a disciplined principle of law with definite limits within which it was to function. The case involved must be one which concerns social transactions *(muamalat)* and not one relating to religious observances *(ibadat)*. The interest studied must be in harmony with the spirit of the *Shariah*.

Istishab

Istishab, continuance or permanence, is the principle of equity most often associated with the school of al-Shafii although it was also emphasized by the Hanbalis. The term *istishab* refers to the presumption in the law that conditions known to exist in the past continue to exist or remain valid until proven otherwise. For example, a missing person *(mafqud)* is presumed to be alive until the opposite is proved, either through proof of his demise or a judicial decree to that effect based on the elapsing of the number of years necessary to complete a normal life span.

The history of Islamic law contains numerous examples in

which Muslim sovereigns interpreted and enacted laws in view of justice or the general welfare. Such actions were founded in the very sources of law *(usul al-fiqh)*, the *Quran, Sunnah* of the Prophet and *ijma.*

CONCLUSION

The early Muslims' religious vision of realizing the Will of God in history inspired not only the vast geographical expansion of Islam but also the early development of Islamic law. This concern about knowing God's Will in order to implement it produced classical Muslim law. The science of Muslim jurisprudence within these first centuries devised both the sources of law *(usul al-fiqh)* and substantive law itself *(furu al-fiqh)*. As we have seen, according to classical legal theory that has predominated down to the twentieth century, in the development of law, four sources of jurisprudence were employed: the *Quran, Sunnah* of the Prophet, *qiyas,* and *ijma.* Laws were derived from the revealed texts of the *Quran* and the *Sunnah,* or from the product of the jurists' analogical reasoning based upon these texts. The authority for their interpretations came from what was considered the infallible *ijma* of the scholars. At the same time, there was recognition within the schools themsleves of subsidiary principles of equity previously described *(istihsan, istislah,* and *istishab).*

However, due to a number of factors, the interaction of these sources and the continued dynamism of legal development after the tenth century were stifled. A series of events were to gradually stop this creative process: "the closing of the door of *ijtihad,*" growing political fragmentation and decay, assimilated customs contrary to the *Quranic* spirit, and finally the Mongol invasions of the thirteenth century. All played a part in halting creative legal activity.

The relationship of *ijtihad* and *ijma* had, during the formative period of law, been a dynamic one in which the fresh *ijtihad* (interpretation) of the scholar was either accepted or rejected by the community. In the tenth century, however, the consensus of the majority of legal scholars determined that the elaboration of law was complete. Independent interpretation was deemed to be no longer necessary and so the door of *ijtihad* was closed. Henceforth, the role of jurists was to follow or imitate *(taqlid)* the established authoritative doctrines of the law schools. Thus, in the tenth century, not only was *ijtihad* restricted, but the dynamic relationship between *ijtihad* and *ijma* was severed. *Ijma* became the infallible consensus of scholars and as such, functioned in legal theory as an instrument of legal conservatism.

The effect of this conservatism is reflected in the legal literature of the period which consisted of exhaustive commentaries on the principal works of the great *Imams* of the past such as Abu Hanifa, Malik, al-Shafii, and ibn Hanbal. These legal handbooks contained the principal teachings of each school of law and served as authoritative reference works for the *qadis* (judges) who applied the law.

Among the other factors that contributed to Muslim conservatism was the growing political fragmentation of the Abbasid Caliphate from the middle of the tenth century, a gradual decentralization into small semi-autonomous feudal states. This period of political decline was accompanied by a growing moral and social decay as the Muslim ruling class, in addition to its earlier absorptions of Byzantine and Persian governmental institutions, assimilated many of their less savory practices — large harems, concubines, and most importantly for women's role in the family, the customs of veiling and seclusion.[5]

The political weakness that had begun in the middle of the tenth century, and had led to the steady decline of the Abbasid dynasty, culminated in its collapse in 1258 at the hands of the Mongols. The Mongol invaders led by Hulagu Khan destroyed the cultural centers of the eastern Muslim world, including mosque-universities and libraries, as well as hundreds of thousands of its inhabitants. The response of the Muslim community amidst this collapse was a withdrawal into a conservatism that resisted further change. Unfortunately, many of the practices of the time, which had resulted from acculturation of foreign customs and were contrary to *Quranic* values, were already associated with religion, and these too were preserved. This reaction, coupled with the "closing of the door of *ijtihad*" in law, resulted in the relative stagnation of the Muslim community and its jurisprudence.

The sum total of these causes of conservatism was the rather static Muslim society and law in the medieval period. This situation persisted up to the twentieth century when significant changes occurred in Muslim society. The results of such change have been fresh calls for Islamic reform and a revival of the dynamism in law as seen in modern family law reforms passed and proposed which will be discussed in Chapters 3 and 4.

2

CLASSICAL MUSLIM FAMILY LAW

AMILY LAW, WHICH INCLUDES SUCH IMPORTANT AREAS as marriage, divorce and succession, has enjoyed pride of place within the Shariah, a prominence that reflects the Quranic concern for the rights of women and the family. Thus, the traditional family social structure as well as the roles and responsibilities of its members and family values, may be identified in the law.

As noted in the previous chapter, the *Quran* introduced substantial reforms affecting the position of women by creating new regulations and modifying existing customary practice. These *Quranic* reforms, as well as customary practice, constitute the substance of classical family law.

Where *Quranic* reforms and values were incorporated, they served to raise the status of women and the family in Muslim society by establishing the rights of family members. In order to provide a background against which *Quranic* reforms and customary influences can be appreciated, this chapter will begin with a survey of women and the family in pre-Islamic Arabia. This will be followed by a presentation of the major regulations for marriage, divorce, and inheritance in classical family law according to the Hanafi school, which is the official school of Islamic law in the Middle East and South Asia.

WOMEN IN PRE-ISLAMIC ARABIA

Women's status in pre-Islamic Arabia was reflected in the predominant marriage agreement, a contract that closely resembled a sale through which a woman became the property of her husband.[1] She was obliged to follow him to his tribe and to bear children who were considered to be of his blood. The wife's tribe relinquished its rights to her and to her future children by receiving a price or gift called *mahr* (dower). Strong emphasis was placed on the chastity and potential fidelity of the woman. Therefore, her family strictly limited her behavior in order to insure her reputation and consequently the family's honor. Since a woman would eventually leave the family, her value consisted primarily in the dower (*mahr*) her family received at her marriage sale. In addition, any possibility of her right to inheritance from her family, especially inheritance of fixed property such as land, which would in effect be transferring family wealth to another tribe, was out of the question. And, the married woman's status in her new family was not improved. As a wife she became totally subject to her husband and to his kindred and totally dependent upon them for maintenance and support.

The marriage of dominion in ancient Arabia produced a situation in which a woman was subjugated by males, her father, brother or close male relatives when she was a virgin and her husband when she became a wife. As a matter of custom, she came to be regarded as little more than a piece of property.

Women's low status in society is reflected in *Quranic* condemnations, especially regarding female infanticide.

> When news is brought to one of them of [the birth of] a female [child], his face darkens, and he is filled with inward grief! With shame does he hide himself from his people because of the bad news he had had! Shall he retain it [on sufferance and contempt],

or bury it in the dust? Ah! What an evil [choice] they decide on.
(XVI:58–59)[2]

A woman had no voice in her marriage (in its initiation or
in its termination). Another factor contributing to women's inferior
status was men's right of unlimited polygamy, contingent solely
upon the males' ability to capture or purchase women.

The prevalence of marriage agreements which led to the
general denial of any rights for women in marriage, divorce and
inheritance provides the social context against which the life of the
Prophet and the revelation of the *Quran* must be understood in
order to see the profound social changes wrought by Islam.

Islam brought a shift in the basis of the social foundation—
from blood kinship to fellowship in a community *(ummah)* of
believers, from loyalty to the tribe to that of the extended family as
its basic unit. A strong family meant recognition not only of male
rights but of female rights as well. This realization can be seen in
family law reforms in the areas of marriage, divorce and inheritance. Quranic injunctions, intended to raise women's status and
equality, represented some of the most radical departures from
customary law in ancient Arabia. Classical family law as finally
formulated was the product of Quranic reform and customary
practice.

MARRIAGE

Why Marriage?

The central role of marriage in Islam is well illustrated by the
Prophet's oft-quoted expression that "There shall be no monkery
in Islam." Islam considers marriage, which is an important
safeguard for chastity, to be incumbent on every Muslim man and
woman unless they are physically or financially unable to lead
conjugal life. Through marriage, the Muslim engages in an activity
that is life-affirming rather than life-denying. Marriage is central to
the growth and stability of the basic unit of society, the Muslim
family, the means by which the world is populated with Muslims to

concretize and realize God's Will in history. Physically, the labor of men is needed to spread the faith and to fight for it.

Definition of Marriage

Marriage (*nikah*) in Islam is recognized as a highly religious sacred covenant. However, it is not religious in the sense of a sacrament, but rather in the sense of realizing the essence of Islam. In Islamic law, it is a civil contract legalizing intercourse and the procreation of children. Marriage, reflecting the practical bent of Islam, combines the nature of both *ibadat* (worship) and *muamalat* (social relations).

Essential Requirements of Marriage

The contract of marriage considerably raised the status of a woman in pre-Islamic Arabia by making her a party to the marriage agreement rather than an object for sale. A Muslim man or woman who is of sound mind and who has attained puberty (twelve years of age for boys and nine for girls)[3] is considered to have the legal capacity to contract a valid marriage for himself or herself or as a guardian for others. Since it was customary in an agrarian society to marry at an early age, the allowance of marriage at puberty was appropriate to the social situation. Great emphasis was placed on the value of many children which a young wife with many child-bearing years ahead could more easily provide.

The law does not require any particular form or ceremony in which the contractual agreement must be made, nor does it require any evidence of the union in writing. The custom of oral contracts seems to have prevailed although the *Quran* does recommend that such an agreement be in written form: "Disdain not to reduce to writing [your contract] for a future period... it is juster in the sight of God, more suitable as evidence, and more convenient to prevent doubts among yourselves" (II:282).

Essential to the marriage is the offer (*ijab*) of one contracting party and the acceptance (*qabul*) of the other, occurring at the same meeting before two witnesses. In Islamic law, by *Quranic* provision, the place of one male witness may be taken by two female witnesses: "And get two witnesses, . . . and if there are not two men, then a man and two women, such as ye choose, for witnesses, so that if one of them errs the other can remind her" (II:282). The higher social regard for men as witnesses in worldly affairs is reflected in the above regulation. This higher regard for men results in granting them more extensive rights in the law. In laws governing the arrangement of marriage for minors, the rights of men and women as well as boys and girls, as will be seen in the following, differ considerably.

Guardianship in Marriage

A distinguishing feature of Islamic law is the power *(jabr)* that it bestows upon the father or grandfather who can contract a valid marriage for minors which cannot be annulled at puberty. The right of guardianship is known as *wilayat* and the guardian is a *wali*. The inability of minors to repudiate the marriage seems to rest on the jurists' assumption that fathers and grandfathers who are fond of their offspring would not have sinister motives in arranging their marriages. However, this regulation is not supported by any *Quranic* prescription or *Sunnah* of the Prophet. If the marriage was contracted negligently or fraudulently, or by someone other than the father or grandfather, it can be repudiated by the minor when he or she attains puberty. This is called "option of puberty" *(khiyar al-bulugh)*. The option applies to all marriages contracted by those other than the father or grandfather, even the minor's mother, who, as a woman, may be "deficient in judgment."[4]

Lack of confidence in a woman's judgment is an attitude (also reflected in Western countries for many centuries) that probably resulted from the strict division of labor and social activity in Muslim society. The woman who spent most of her life engaged in domestic duties, completely segregated from the world of legal and business agreements, came to be viewed as less competent to deal with such matters. Thus, one can see the influence of custom and traditional attitudes upon the law. Among the many illustrations found in family law are the rules governing the "option of puberty." This option is lost to the virgin female who has reached puberty if she does nothing or if she merely remains silent for what is considered a reasonable time after she has been informed of the marriage and of her option. However, the option is preserved for the boy under the same circumstances. His right continues until he actively approves the marriage or implies approval by the act of payment of dower or by actual cohabitation.[5]

If the husband or wife does exercise the option to repudiate, it must be confirmed by the court. Until this is done, the marriage continues, and if either party should die in the interval, the other would inherit from him or her.

Classification of Marriage

Like all other contracts, marriage has certain qualifications. However, unless its most basic requirements are violated, its validity remains. Marriages are classified by the degree of their validity as (a) *batil,* void, completely bad in its foundations; (b) *fasid,* irregular, good in its foundations but unlawful in its attributes; and (c) *sahih,* valid and completely lawful. As will be indicated, those marriage partners who do not fulfill all legal requirements for a *sahih* marriage are, in turn, denied many important legal rights.

Batil Marriage

A *batil* (void) marriage is an unlawful union that awards no mutual rights to the partners and imposes no obligations. The death of one partner does not entitle the other to any inheritance. Since the marriage is null and void and thus not considered to exist, the offspring are illegitimate. *Batil* marriages include such situations as marriage of a Muslim woman to more than one husband at the same time, or a marriage prohibited on the grounds of consanguinity (blood relationship through a male ancestor), affinity (marital relationship), or fosterage.

Fasid Marriage

A *fasid* marriage is irregular because of (1) lack of a formality that may be rectified, as in the case of a secret marriage or a marriage contracted with less than the legal number of witnesses, or (2) an impediment that can be removed, as when a husband already has four wives. If a judge *(qadi)* is made aware of such an irregular marriage, he, as guardian of the law of God, must either legalize or terminate the relationship.

An irregular marriage has no legal effect until it is consummated, and even after consummation, the rights of the partners are limited. The wife has the right of dower but no right of maintenance. Furthermore, there are no mutual rights of inheritance. The children of this marriage are considered legitimate, however, and are entitled to a share of the inheritance. To dissolve the relationship, only a single declaration of divorce is necessary. One of the partners at any time need only say "I have relinquished you" to annul the contract.

Sahih Marriage

A *sahih* (sound or valid) marriage conforms to every requirement of the law and is not affected by prohibitions in the *batil* marriages or in *fasid* marriages. The partners of a *sahih* marriage are entitled to all of the rights and subject to all of the obligations of a valid marriage.

Competency of the Parties in a Marriage

The various requirements which determine the classification of a marriage center around the following areas: (1) number of spouses, (2) religion, (3) family relationship, (4) *iddah*, and (5) equality.

Number of Spouses

A Muslim man may have up to four wives. This law represents another reform raising the status of women who had been subjected to unlimited polygamy practiced in pre-Islamic times. Social circumstances during this period must be kept in mind: the widely-accepted practice of polygamy and the existence of many widows and orphans left by men who had died in battle who were in need of protection through marriage. The *Quranic* verse from which the control of polygamy is derived must be understood in the context of problems resulting from the battle of Uhud (625) which had caused the deaths of a substantial percentage of Muslim men: "If ye fear that ye shall not be able to deal justly with the orphans, marry women of your choice, two or three, or four; But if ye fear that ye shall not be able to deal justly [with them] then only one" (IV: 3).

Because of the patrilineal social structure through which children belonged to the male's family, a Muslim woman was only permitted to marry one husband at a time so that the paternity of her children could be established. If she married a second husband, this marriage was considered to be completely void. In addition, her children from the second husband were illegitimate and were therefore excluded from inheritance. They could not be legitimized by any later acknowledgement.

Religion

Under Hanafi law a Muslim man is allowed to marry a Muslim woman, or a Jewish or Christian woman (kitabiyyah) who believes in a heavenly or revealed religion which has a *kitab* or revealed book. He cannot, however, marry an idolatress or a fire-worshipper. A Muslim woman, again more controlled in the exercise of her options, can marry only a Muslim man.[6]

Family Relationship

Prohibitions of marriage based on family relationship are derived from the *Quran* (IV:23). Marriages are prohibited for partners who have a certain blood relationship or consanguinity. Thus, a man may not marry his ascendants h.h.s. (how high soever), or descendants h.l.s. (how low soever).[7]

A man is also prohibited from marriage with relations by affinity, that is, the ascendants h.h.s. or descendants h.l.s. of his wife (provided his marriage to this wife was consummated) or the wife of an ascendant h.h.s. or descendant h.l.s. Also prohibited is a marriage where the relationship of fosterage exists, as for example, marriage with one's foster-sister, foster-mother, or her daughter.

Another barrier to marriage in the category of family relationship involved unlawful conjunction. A Muslim must not be married at the same time to women related by consanguinity, affinity, or fosterage, as for example, two sisters or an aunt and her niece. An unlawful union in Hanafi law renders a marriage irregular but not void.[8]

Iddah

In Hanafi law, a woman is prohibited from remarrying for a specified period of time called the *iddah* (waiting period) when her previous marriage has been terminated by divorce or by the death of her husband. *Iddah* is defined as the term by the completion of which a new marriage, if contracted, would be lawful. During *iddah* a woman must remain in seclusion in order to ascertain whether she is pregnant by her husband, and thus avoid any confusion of parentage. As will be discussed later, the *iddah* period served a number of purposes. In addition to determining parentage, it was a period for reconciliation and required payment of maintenance. If a marriage was not consummated, *iddah* need not be observed except in the case of a husband's death, since consummation may be the subject of conflicting claims of paternity, inheritance, and maintenance.

If the marriage is consummated before it is dissolved by divorce, the duration of the *iddah* is three menstrual cycles. If the woman is pregnant, the *iddah* continues until her delivery. If the marriage is terminated by the husband's death, the *iddah* period is four months, ten days from the death of the husband. If, at the conclusion of this period, the widow is pregnant, her *iddah* continues until delivery of the child.

The prohibitions of *iddah* after divorce extend to the husband, who may not marry again during the period of his former wife's *iddah*. However, marriage before the completion of the *iddah* is not considered void, but merely irregular. To determine consummation of the marriage, which is a key issue in the practice of *iddah*, valid retirement *(al-khalwah al-sahihah)* can be used. To prove valid retirement, the husband and wife must have privacy and there must be no reason to prevent marital intercourse. Valid retirement also has the same effect as consummation not only in determining *iddah*, but also in confirming the right to dower, in establishing paternity, and in assessing the wife's right to maintenance.

Equality

A somewhat less important doctrine regarding marriage is *kafaah*, the rule of equality which states that a marriage is a suitable union in law if the man is equal in social status to the woman. However, this obligation does not apply to the woman, since she is considered to be raised to the husband's position by marriage. In Hanafi law, equality is a necessary condition determined by (1) family, (2) Islam, (3) profession, (4) freedom, (5) good character, and (6) means. A marriage that does not favorably meet these criteria is not necessarily void. The judge *(qadi)* must carefully exercise his discretion in determining whether to annul the marriage *(faskh)* on the basis that it was a mésalliance.

Consequences of Marriage (Rights and Obligations of Partners)

Once the essential requirements for a valid marriage have been fulfilled, the marriage agreement imposes specific obligations and insures specific rights for each marriage partner. Among the most significant rights and obligations are those concerning obedience, regulation of marriage agreements, property rights, dower, maintenance, guardianship, and parentage.

Duties of the Wife

The wife's main obligation involves maintaining a home, caring for her children, and obeying her husband. He is entitled to exercise his marital authority by restraining his wife's movements and preventing her from showing herself in public. This restriction of the wife mirrors the prevailing medieval social customs of veiling and seclusion of women, practiced in order to protect their honor.

Regulations of Marriage Agreements

In many cases, the rights awarded to a woman as a legal entity contributed significantly to her rise in status in comparison to her pre-Islamic state. One important right granted in the Hanbali (but not Hanafi) school, which in modern times is recognized as a means by which women can obtain a considerable measure of independence and status in marriage, concerns the partners' ability to regulate agreements in a contract by adding clauses containing additional provisions to the marriage contract as shall be seen, this approach has been employed by modern reforms. Agreements can be formed at the time of the marriage or afterwards and are valid and enforceable provided that they are not contrary to the policy of the law. Conditions that are contrary to the object of marriage (for example, clauses saying that the wife need not live with her husband or that the husband need not maintain his wife) would be void, although the marriage would still be valid. However, clauses that extend the natural consequences of marriage, such as a husband's promise to maintain his wife in a certain life style, are valid.

This right granted by the Hanbali school can considerably raise the status of the wife in a marital relationship. Her ability to make additional conditions not automatically arising from the marriage contract, but also not contrary to the object of marriage, can solve many inequities in such areas as polygamy or divorce. For example, clauses may be added to the contract that eliminate the husband's right to take a second wife. Clauses may also grant the wife a greater amount of freedom of movement. These stipulations limit the husband's somewhat automatic and extensive legal control of his wife. And, since these conditions can be enforced by granting the wife her husband's power of divorce if they are violated, more equal rights of divorce are granted to the wife.

Property Rights

Although both parties inherit from each other, neither acquires interest in the property of a spouse because of the marriage. This principle was the result of a *Quranic* reform (IV:7) which gave the woman the right to own and manage property herself and to keep possession of this property even after her marriage.

Dower Rights

Another right granted to the woman as a result of *Quranic* prescription is her right to dower *(mahr)*, intended to safeguard her economic position after marriage. Dower is considered to be essential in every marriage contract. It may be defined as a payment which the wife is entitled to receive from the husband in consideration of the marriage. As the *Quran* specifies: "And give the women [on marriage] their dower as a free gift" (IV:4). In pre-Islamic Arabia the word *sadaq* represented the husband's gift to his wife, while dower *(mahr)* was paid to the bride's father. However, Islamic law made dower payable not to the bride's father, but only to the bride herself. Like the contract itself, this action also made the woman a party to the contract and so the marriage agreement could not be considered a sale.

Dower could also be used as a means for controlling the husband's power of divorce, since upon dissolution of the marriage he is required to pay the total amount of the dower at once. In cases where the wife is divorced before consummation of the marriage, she has the right to one-half of her agreed-upon dower or, in Hanafi law, if there is no agreed-upon dower, she is entitled to a gift of three articles of dress or their value. Such provisions are also derived from the *Quran:* "There is no blame on you if ye divorce women before consummation or the fixation of their dower; but bestow on them [a suitable gift]" (II:236), and "And if ye divorce them before consummation but after fixation of a dower for them, then half of the dower [is due to them]" (II:237).

Dower may be classified into several categories. The first, specified dower (al-mahr al-musamma), is usually fixed on the occasion of the marriage and recorded in a register by the qadi performing the ceremony. The amount of dower fixed by the father for his minor son binds the son for the amount, but in Hanafi law the father himself is not liable for payment.

Unspecified or proper dower (mahr al-mithl) refers to an amount that has not been fixed. Although it may not be specified, dower is a legal responsibility not dependent upon any contract between the parties. If dower is not determined, the amount will be decided by the social position of the bride's father's family as well as her own qualifications, such as those cited by the Hedaya: age, beauty, fortune, understanding, and virtue. The amounts of dower set for other females in the bride's family will also be a determinant, but the husband's social or financial position is not a consideration.

The practice of dividing dower into two portions, prompt (muqaddam) and deferred (muakhkhar), is universal in the Hanafi school. Prompt dower is payable upon conclusion of the marriage contract and deferred dower must be paid only on termination of the marriage and thus, as mentioned above, serves as a bona fide protection in the event of a divorce.

The wife's claim for the unpaid portion of her dower is legally considered an unsecured debt ranking equally with other unsecured debts due from her husband or, after his death, from his estate. The wife is entitled to receive the debt herself or if she predeceases her husband, her heirs, including the husband, are entitled to the dower.

Under Muslim law a widow whose dower has not been paid is entitled to the "widow's right of retention" which enables her to retain (but not obtain) possession of her husband's estate until her debt is paid. However, her unpaid debt does not make her the owner of this property.

The guardian of a minor wife whose husband refuses to pay prompt dower may refuse to send the wife to her husband's house. In addition, before consummation, the wife may refuse conjugal rights until dower is paid. Under these circumstances if she lives outside of his house, the husband must nevertheless maintain her. However, the wife loses her right to refuse herself once consummation or co-habitation occur.

These elaborately developed laws for the husband's payment of the dower to his wife represent one part of his monetary obligations to the women in his family. In fact, this sum was often received by the bridegroom from his father or grandfather who, as the traditional head of the extended family, controlled all family wealth. In traditional times, not only payment of dower, but also the other extensive monetary obligations of the male for all his womenfolk were collectively born by the many male members of his close-knit family group, who often lived in the same household. Women in the family who were secluded, veiled, and restricted from most aspects of public life did not earn their own living. This role was traditionally reserved exclusively for the males, a role fulfilled as a point of honor. Women without an independent means of support were necessarily extensively protected through the legal maintenance obligations of their male kin.

Maintenance Rights

Maintenance (*nafaqah*), another important obligation of the husband, includes food, clothing, and lodging. Maintenance is the husband's primary obligation, regardless of his wife's private means. The wife has first preference for maintenance over her children. The husband's obligation begins when his wife reaches puberty and continues unless she refuses him conjugal rights or is otherwise disobedient since, in return for her maintenance, the wife owes the husband her faithfulness and obedience. However, if her behavior is caused by non-payment of prompt dower or the necessity of leaving her husband's house because of his cruelty, maintenance must still be paid.

A wife is also entitled to maintenance during the period of *iddah* following a divorce, and if she ceases to menstruate before the completion of this *iddah* period, the wife is entitled to maintenance until she completes three menstrual cycles. This ruling is intended to protect women who may be pregnant. However, a widow does not receive maintenance during the *iddah* following her husband's death since maintenance is considered to be inconsistent with her position as an heir.

If the husband refuses to pay maintenance, the wife has the right to sue for it. The various schools of law have defined the extent of her rights in this situation in different ways. The Hanafi school shows more preference for the male in that it does not allow the wife the right to past maintenance unless a distinct agreement was previously made. The wife who, after a period of time, sues for maintenance, has no means to obtain payment of her husband's past-due debt. In contrast, the Shafii and Hanbali schools consider maintenance arrears to be the husband's ongoing debt which can be claimed regardless of the amount of time that has elapsed.

In classical Hanafi law, the wife is put at a further disadvantage economically by the fact that neither inability, refusal, nor neglect to maintain are considered to be sufficient grounds for the dissolution of her marriage. This is contrary to the principles of both the Maliki and the Shafii schools. The hardships resulting from the traditional Hanafi position are numerous. For example, a wife, who in traditional society is unable to support herself and her children, is also unable to free herself from a husband who has been imprisoned for a number of years.

A father is also bound to maintain those of his children who belong in the following categories:

1. his infant children whether or not he had custody of them;
2. the infant children of a son who is unable to do so;
3. his disabled son or student son;
4. his unmarried daughter of any age; and
5. his widowed or divorced daughter if she is ill.

If the father is poor, the mother and then the paternal grandfather are bound to maintain the children.[9]

Maintenance is not required of a father-in-law for a widowed daughter-in-law, and a father is also not bound to maintain his illegitimate children.

The close ties between members of the larger family are reflected in the laws governing the maintenance of other relatives. Persons who are not poor are bound to maintain their poor relatives. The maintenance required should be determined in proportion to the share which they would inherit from these relatives at their death.

Parentage

Parentage is established in Islam by birth during a regular or irregular, but not a void marriage, or by the father's acknowledgement. Thus, the child's rights to legitimacy are at times dependent upon the good will of his father. A child's legitimacy determines both his rights to maintenance and to inheritance from his father.

Legitimacy is determined in classical Islamic law by the following rules: (1) A child who is born within six months of a marriage is considered illegitimate unless the father acknowledges him. (2) A child who is born after six months of marriage is considered legitimate unless the father disclaims him. (3) After the dissolution of the marriage, a child is considered legitimate if born within two years (in Hanafi law).[10]

The father's acknowledgement of paternity (*iqrar*) is possible and effective under the following conditions: (1) when the father of a child is not known to be anyone else; (2) if the man could, at the time the child was conceived, have been the husband of the mother [this implies that it has not been provided that the child was conceived by illicit intercourse (*zina*) and that the alleged marriage has not been disproved]; (3) if the ages of the parties are appropriate for that of father and son; and (4) if the acknowledgment is not only of sonship but of legitimate sonship.[11]

DIVORCE

Why Divorce?

Because marriage in Islam is the basis of society, the means by which the race is perpetuated, it has always been viewed by Sunni Muslims as a permanent institution. Contrary to pre-Islamic practice, temporary marriages *(mutah)* are forbidden. The prophet is reported to have said that "of all the permitted things, divorce is the most abominable with God." As will be seen, many verses in the *Quran* seek to limit both the frequency and the facility of divorce in pre-Islamic Arabia.

The negative attitudes toward divorce in Islam are clearly reflected in the opinions of Hanafi jurists. As the *Hedaya* states, divorce is: "a dangerous and disapproved procedure as it dissolves marriage, an institution which involves many circumstances as well of a temporal as of a spiritual nature; nor is its propriety at all admitted, but on the ground of urgency of release from an unsuitable wife."[12]

However, consistent with its view of marriage as a contract, freely entered by the two parties, provisions were made for legal action to protect the rights of each partner if the terms of the contract were not met. Every attempt should be made to maintain a marriage, but once the marriage becomes a failure, Muslim law allows the parties to separate from one another. Divorce in Islam serves as a safety valve in cases where the spouses can no longer live in harmony and so the very purpose of marriage would be defeated if they remained together.

Definition of Divorce

Divorce is generally referred to as *talaq,* meaning "repudiation." *Talaq* comes from the root *tallaqa* meaning to release a human being from any obligation incumbent upon him. It signifies one spouse's release of the other spouse from the marriage bond, whether by repudiation or legal process.

As will be seen in the forthcoming discussion, the attitudes of the *Quran* regarding the necessary control of divorce are reflected in the approved forms *(ahsan* and *hasan)* of divorce. In comparison to the completely unbridled rights of husbands to divorce their wives in pre-Islamic Arabia, these approved forms of divorce represented a significant improvement in the treatment of women.

A wife's right to divorce was virtually non-existent in pre-Islamic times. While the *Quran* granted her some judicial relief from undesirable unions, the strong influence of social customs, especially in the Hanafi school of law, succeeded in limiting that relief to very narrow grounds.

Classification of Divorce

Divorce can be classified into five major categories: (1) talaq, (2) talaq al-tafwid, (3) khul or mubaraah, (4) lian and faskh, and (5) apostasy.

Talaq Proper

The first category and the most comprehensive, talaq proper, is the husband's right to divorce his wife by making a pronouncement that the marriage is dissolved. The male's extensive duties in the socio-economic sphere, and thus the dominant position of the husband in the family and society is reflected in some of the consequent legal rights he enjoyed over his wife. This is most clearly illustrated in the Muslim male's rather blanket right of divorce. Many Quranic verses make clear the undesirability of divorce and the punishments awaiting those who exceed the limits set by Allah.[13] The law did not translate these teachings and values of the Quran into specific legal restrictions on the husband's right to divorce to guard against abuses.

Conditional, contingent, or qualified pronouncements of divorce are permitted in Hanafi law. For example, a divorce may be pronounced to take place at the occurrence of some future event or at some future period of time.

The husband's pronouncement of divorce must indicate an intention to divorce, as for example, in the following expressions: "Thou art divorced," or "I have divorced thee," or "I divorce my wife forever and render her haram (forbidden) for me." However, regardless of the verbal meaning, actual intention to divorce is not necessary. Because Hanafi law considers the action to be one of great gravity, if the husband uses the formula of repudiation in jest, in drunkenness, or even under compulsion, it is still considered to be valid and effective.

Although it could cause hardships for wives of impetuous husbands, another consequence of this provision was that it provided wives of undesirable husbands with an unforseen opportunity to dissolve their marriages. For example, in Turkey during the rule of the Sultans a convention developed that allowed a wife to go before a *qadi* with two witnesses and claim that her husband had divorced her when he was drunk, a claim he would be unable to deny.[14]

A husband's act of divorce in Hanafi law is unencumbered. A Muslim who has attained puberty and is of sound mind has the right to divorce his wife whenever he wishes without citing a cause. The fact that the wife has no part in the procedure is further indicated by the fact that she does not have to be present nor must she be informed. The divorce can be either revocable, which gives the man an opportunity to reconsider the decision, or irrevocable. Since the Prophet did not approve of divorce, the revocable form of *talaq* is considered to be the "approved" form. Thus, the forms of *talaq* can be classified into *talaq al-sunnah*, divorce which is in consonance with the Prophet's teachings, and *talaq al-bidah*, divorce which does not follow the Prophet's teachings. This divorce represents an innovation and is therefore unapproved.

Talaq al-sunnah can be divided into two categories. The first is *talaq al-ahsan*, the more proper and orthodox form of divorce and thus the least disapproved. This takes place during the period of *tuhr* ("purity"—the time when a woman is not experiencing menstruation). If a woman is beyond the age of menstruation or if the parties have been separated for a long time, *tuhr* may be dispensed with. With the *ahsan* divorce, the husband utters a single pronouncement and then abstains from sexual intercourse with his wife during her *iddah*. The pronouncement is revocable (by words or conduct, as for example, resumed cohabitation) during the whole period of *iddah*. This restriction allowed considerable time for reconsideration of the husband's decision and family arbitration to bring the couple together again, and thus followed the *Quran:* "And their husbands have the better right to take them back in that period, if they wish for reconciliation" (II:228). At the completion of the period, the divorce becomes irrevocable.

The *ahsan* divorce is the most approved form because of the kind and fair treatment given to the wife. The period of suspense for her is not so prolonged as in the second mode. And, since there has been only one pronouncement of divorce, there is no prohibition against re-marriage of the parties. In addition, if the husband or wife dies during the period of *iddah*, the partner still inherits.

The *talaq al-hasan* form of divorce is also approved, although to a lesser degree than the first since it follows the letter but not the spirit of the Prophet's injunctions. The *hasan* divorce is carried out by making three consecutive pronouncements (the first two having been consecutively revoked) during three successive periods of *tuhr*, with no intercourse taking place during any of the three *tuhrs*. The first pronouncement should be made during a *tuhr*, the second during the next *tuhr* and the third during the following *tuhr*. The third pronouncement serves as a final and irrevocable dissolution of the marriage, and thus with it, intercourse becomes unlawful and *iddah* is required. Now re-marriage is impossible unless the wife marries another, consummates the marriage, and is then lawfully divorced.

The third pronouncement is irrevocable to prevent the practice of divorcing a wife and then taking her back several times in order to induce her to purchase her freedom by relinquishing her dower *(mahr)* or making some other financial sacrifice: "A divorce is only permissible twice: after that, the parties should either hold together on equitable terms, or separate with kindness. It is not lawful for you [men], to take back any of your gifts [from your wives]" (II:229).

Unlike the two approved forms of divorce, the following two disapproved forms *(talaq al-bidah)* do not allow for a chance to reconsider a possible capricious or hastily-made decision. These forms of divorce, similar to the husband's unfettered right of divorce in pre-Islamic Arabia, again made their way through the force of custom into common practice and were incorporated into Islamic law. They are valid but disapproved and sinful.

The first disapproved form of divorce, the *talaq al-bidah*, consists of three declarations of divorce occurring at one time. The "triple declaration" is made during a single *tuhr* by pronouncing one sentence, "I divorce thee thrice," or three separate sentences, "I divorce thee; I divorce thee; I divorce thee," and thus the marriage is irrevocably dissolved.

The second version of the *talaq al-bidah* consists of one irrevocable declaration. The single pronouncement can be made in oral or written form during a *tuhr* or even at another time. At the moment of pronouncement or at the writing of the divorce, the marital tie is immediately severed.

The allowance of these two forms in law directly contradicts *Quranic* prescription: "When ye divorce women, divorce them at their prescribed periods, and count (accurately) their prescribed periods, . . . And fear God your Lord. . . . Those are limits set by God: and any who transgress the limits of God, does verily wrong his (own) soul" LXV: 1). However, since Islamic law permitted the *talaq al-bidah*, only the husband's conscience served as a restraint from the use of such disapproved forms of divorce.[15]

Talaq al-Tafwid (Delegated Divorce)

The second main category of divorce is *talaq al-tafwid*. In traditional Muslim law, while a husband enjoys an almost unilateral right to divorce, a wife's ability to divorce is very limited, a restriction that mirrors women's dependent role in society. It fails to reflect verses in the *Quran* which indicate a wider range of divorce options for the wife. For example: "And women shall have rights similar to those against them, according to what is equitable" (II:228).

One power of the wife to divorce, strictly controlled by her husband, is *talaq al-tafwid* (delegated divorce). Here, the power of divorce is delegated to her by her husband when he expresses such words as "choose" or "divorce yourself."

Khul and Mubaraah (Mutual Divorce)

A *Khul* divorce comes about through the common consent of the wife and the husband: "If ye (judges) do indeed fear that they would be unable to keep the limits ordained by God, there is no blame on either of them if she give something for her freedom" (II:229). This mutual consent includes the wife's giving some compensation (part or all of her dower) to her husband. However, awarding the dower is not absolutely necessary. A *khul* repudiation can also take place without payment of compensation by the wife.

Mutual divorce may take two forms: the above-mentioned *khul* if the desire to separate is expressed by the wife, or *mubaraah* when both mutually want a separation. According to Hanafi law, the correct procedure for divorce takes place at one meeting when the husband proposes dissolution and the wife accepts it. Once the offer is accepted, in both the *khul* and *mabaraah* divorces, it operates as a single irrevocable divorce.

Lian and *Faskh* (Divorce by Judicial Process)

Dissolution of marriage may also be brought about by judicial process. The first type in this category is *lian* (mutual oath swearing). Here the husband alleges without legal proof that his wife has committed adultery. The wife then is entitled to file suit to bring about a retraction of her husband's statement or the swearing of an oath by her husband that she is guilty of adultery. His insistence upon her guilt under oath would thus bring the wrath of God upon him if he has accused her falsely. Once the wife has filed suit, intercourse with her husband becomes unlawful unless he retracts his claim. The swearing of the oaths in *lian* are governed by regulations in the *Quran:*

> And for those who launch a charge against their spouses, and have (in support) no evidence but their own, — their solitary evidence (can be received) if they bear witness four times (with an oath) by God that they are solemnly telling the truth; and the fifth (oath) (should be) that they solemnly invoke the curse of God on themselves if they tell a lie. But it would avert the punishment from the wife, if she bears witness four times (with an oath) by God, that (her husband) is telling a lie; And the fifth (oath) should be that she solemnly invokes the wrath of God on herself if (her accuser) is telling the truth (XXIV:6–9).

After the oaths of both husband and wife have been made, the husband can divorce his wife. If he refuses to do so if the parties have not agreed to forgive each other, the court must dissolve the marriage. This has the same effect as one irrevocable *talaq*. A second form of divorce involving judicial process is known as *faskh*, judicial recision of a marriage contract. *Faskh* (annulment or abrogation) means "to annul" (a deed) or "to rescind" (a bargain). In family law it refers to the power of the Muslim *qadi* to annul a marriage on the petition of the wife. The grounds that are available to women seeking divorce in the Hanafi school are both limited in number and difficult to prove. In contrast, as we have seen, the husband is required by law to cite no grounds whatever to validate his repudiation of his wife.

The schools of law differ considerably in the number and kinds of grounds available to women who wish to divorce. The Maliki school, followed by the Shafii and Hanbali schools is the most liberal. The Hanafi school is the narrowest. In Hanafi law, a court may dissolve a marriage only if: (1) the marriage is irregular; (2) a person who has the option to dissolve the marriage exercises it; (3) the parties are prohibited from marriage by fosterage; (4) the marriage was contracted by non-Muslims who subsequently adopt Islam (or vice versa); (5) a husband is unable to consummate the marriage; or (6) he is missing. In the latter case, the court can declare the marriage ended after a period of time, enabling it to presume that the wife is a widow (putative widowhood). However, the wife must wait for a divorce for a period of ninety years from the date of her husband's birth.

In contrast to the Hanafi school, the more liberal Maliki school allowed a wife to divorce on the grounds of her husband's (1) cruelty; (2) refusal or inability to maintain her; (3) desertion; or (4) serious disease or ailment that would make a continuance of the marriage harmful to the wife. As will be seen in Chapter III, modern reform legislation looked to Maliki law to expand a wife's grounds for divorce.

Divorce by Apostasy or Conversion

In the Hanafi school, a husband's and wife's renunciation of Islam (apostasy) whether or not the marriage was consummated, dissolves the marital tie, *ipso facto*. Because this condition also provides a possible opportunity for wives to dissolve their marriage, cases can be found in which wives would claim to have committed apostasy in order to free themselves from their husbands.[16]

Consequences of Divorce (Rights and Obligations of Partners)

Following a divorce, certain rights and obligations of both parties come into effect.

Iddah

The wife's main obligation rests in her observation of *iddah* (waiting period) so that if she is pregnant, no question will occur regarding the paternity of her child and his right to inherit from his father. In addition, her observation of *iddah* provides a period during which a reconciliation may take place.

Dower

Considering the husband's unilateral right to divorce and the potential wrong to which the wife is exposed, *Quranic* verses cite many conditions granting the wife compensation once the divorce is carried out, and these were incorporated into the law. If the marriage was not consummated, the wife is entitled to a suitable gift, if the amount of dower had not been fixed, or one-half of the agreed-upon dower (II:236–237). If the marriage was consummated, the total amount of dower is due immediately.

Maintenance

During the period of her *iddah* the wife is entitled to maintenance from her husband, and this right continues, if she is pregnant, until the birth of her child. Furthermore, if the divorced wife has a young child, she can nurse him for two years. During this period, the father must maintain both mother and child (II:233).

Inheritance

Spouses may inherit from each other if their divorce is revocable. However, rights of inheritance terminate in the case of an irrevocable divorce.

Custody

In Hanafi law, the divorced mother has the right to the custody *(hadanah)* of her male child until he is seven years old and of her female child until puberty, set at age nine. During this time, however, the father, who is legally considered to be the children's natural guardian and maintainer, continues in his supervision of the children and at ages seven and nine he or his paternal relatives receive custody of them.

The awarding of custody to the father is a consistent social reflection of the workings of a traditional, patriarchal, patrilocal family. The family emphasizes the paternal line of ancestry and makes the central residence the home of the paternal grandfather where many women (aunts, grandmother) are available within the family to care for them. However, such laws do not allow much consideration for the children's now-divorced mother whose roles of wife and mother, the main source of a woman's status in a traditional society, may be taken away from her even though she was given no choice in the divorce action. In addition, if she marries another man, custody of her children, regardless of age, is given to her first husband as long as he is an able and proper guardian. A woman loses custody of her child at any age if her behavior is immoral or if she gives the child poor care.

The collective responsibility of extended family members for each other can be seen in the following assignment of relatives responsible for the child. Such a list illustrates the exact assignment of duties for each relative, paralleling the exact assignments of their own maintenance and inheritance rights.

In the absence of or disqualification of the mother, female relatives in the following order receive custody: (1) mother's mother h.h.s.; (2) father's mother h.h.s.; and (3) full sister or other female relatives, including aunts. In the default of female relations, the following male relatives obtain the right of custody: (1) father; (2) nearest paternal grandfather; (3) full brother; (4) consanguine brother; and (5) full brother's son and other paternal relations (in the order of the nearest male relative determined in the same order as that of inheritance).[17] However, no male relative may obtain custody of a female minor unless he is related within the prohibited degrees of consanguinity. If no qualified guardians exist, the court appoints a guardian for the minor.

Reconciliation and Re-marriage

The rules governing the process of reconciliation and re-marriage of the spouses reveal the *Quran's* emphasis upon the importance of marriage and the gravity of divorce. Regulations seek to encourage reconciliation and re-marriage while at the same time discouraging the divorce which had made a re-marriage necessary in the first place.

If, after divorce, reconciliation and re-marriage are desired, the parties are subject to the following regulations. If the husband has made one or two declarations of divorce in the two approved forms *(talaq al-sunnah)* following *Quranic* prescriptions, a reconciliation—either a formal revocation of the repudiation *(talaq)* or resumption of conjugal life—can take place during the *iddah* (waiting) period. Therefore, formal re-marriage is not required. Every possible allowance is made after an approved divorce is carried out to rescind that divorce and quickly re-establish married life again. However, when one or two declarations in the approved forms have been made and the *iddah* period has expired, a regular re-marriage is necessary. In this situation, the gravity of divorce is emphasized by requiring a complete renewal of the marriage agreement.

When three declarations have occurred, the divorce is final and irrevocable, reconciliation and/or remarriage are prohibited. A husband who has pronounced a triple repudiation can only remarry his ex-wife if she marries another and that marriage is terminated through the death of her spouse or through divorce.

The intent of these requirements, which originate in the Quran (II:229), is aimed at curtailing such pre-Islamic practices as perpetually divorcing a wife, pretending to take her back, and then divorcing her again in order to either convince her to relinquish her dower for her final freedom, or to prevent her from re-marrying and seeking the protection of another husband. The damage to his pride which a husband in traditional society must endure in order to re-marry his wife after an irrevocable divorce was doubtless intended to serve as a strong deterrent against hastily-conceived divorces.

SUCCESSION

Why Inheritance?

The customary laws dealing with inheritance in pre-Islamic Arabia were designed to keep property within the individual tribe in order to preserve its strength and power. Inheritance passed only to mature male (agnate) relatives who could also fight and defend their possessions. Male minors were totally excluded. Widows, who were regarded as part of the estate, and daughters, who would no longer belong to the family once they were married, were also barred from inheritance.

The inheritance provisions in the *Quran* modified this system in order to correct injustices. Islam brought a change in the social structure. Loyalty to the Islamic community *(ummah)* transcended tribal allegiance. In the Islamic community, more emphasis was placed upon family ties between husband, wife, and children. The consequent shift in allegiance from the individual tribe to the individual family unit significantly raised the status of women in the society. This Islamic reform is mirrored in the new Quranically stipulated rules of inheritance that were superimposed upon certain unjust customary laws. The *Quran* granted rights of inheritance to the husband and the wife, to children, and to a number of close female relatives who had previously had no rights of succession at all. These new *"Quranic* heirs" received fixed proportions from the deceased's estate before the inheritance passed to the close male relatives. Generally speaking, female heirs were awarded a share equal to one-half that of their male counterparts, whose heavy maintenance responsibilities also cited in the *Quran* justified their larger share. However, where the parents, and uterine brothers and sisters of the deceased are only entitled to a small share of inheritance, men and women share equally in the estate. In addition, no reference is made in the *Quran* to primogeniture. Thus, all sons, regardless of age, received an equal portion of inheritance.

The reforms introduced by the *Quran*, however, did not replace the existing legal scheme. Instead, the customary laws and *Quranic* reforms were fused into a comprehensive and coherent legal structure by the efforts of jurists and the force of events. The system of inheritance that resulted represents a feat of juristic achievement. The Prophet is reported to have said that the laws of inheritance comprise "half the sum of *ilm*" (true knowledge stemming from divine revelation).

Definition of Inheritance

The system of inheritance is the science of duties or obligations *(ilm al-faraid)*; specifically, religious obligations. The reform of customary law through its modification by *Quranic* verses (its Islamicization) will be seen in the explanation of classical laws of inheritance that follows. The outline arranging the structure of priority in inheritance demonstrates both the structure of the traditional extended family and the Islamic concept of social values. Furthermore, it illustrates the meticulous precision with which jurists formulated this elaborate legal system of succession.

Classification of Heirs

Hanafi jurists divide the heirs into seven categories. The first three are the principal classes.

Quranic Heirs

The first class is made up of the *Quranic* heirs *(ahl al-faraid)* whose rights were established by Divine revelation. The

Quranic heirs have been called "Sharers" because they receive a precise fractional share prescribed by the *Quran* (IV:11–12, 176). Although these relatives, who are mostly women, inherit first, they take only a portion of the estate. The strong influence of customary law can be seen by the fact that the residue, usually the bulk of the inheritance, reverts back to the male agnates *(asabah)*.

A list of the twelve relations that make up this first class (Quranic heirs) follows. It includes a treatment of (1) the fraction of the estate which each class of heirs will receive, singly or collectively; (2) those relatives who exclude certain other heirs from inheritance; and (3) the other key circumstances affecting inheritance. The shares mentioned for each heir refer to the net estate, the amount remaining after funeral expenses and other debts have all been paid.

The first two *Quranic* heirs are heirs by "affinity," the *husband and wife*. These heirs always succeed. They do not exclude nor are they excluded by any other relative. If they exist, they reduce the residue that may be taken by the class two relatives (agnates). The husband takes one-fourth of his wife's estate. If his wife has no living children or children of a son h.l.s. (agnatic heirs), he takes one-half.

The wife inherits one-eighth of her husband's estate if there are children or children of a son h.l.s., and one-fourth if there are no children. However, the wife's portion is a collective one. In the case of a polygamous union, the wives share the one-eighth or one-fourth equally. The remainder of the *Quranic* heirs (blood relations) are listed below:

The *father* receives one-sixth. However, when there are children of the deceased or of the deceased's son h.l.s., the father of the deceased is made an agnatic heir.

The *mother* receives one-sixth. However, if there are no children of the deceased, no children of the deceased's son h.l.s., or only one brother or one sister of the deceased, her share is increased to one-third of the whole estate. If the husband or wife as well as the father of the deceased are alive, she will receive one-third of the residue after deducting the husband's or the wife's share.

One *daughter* of the deceased is entitled to one-half of the estate and two or more daughters receive two-thirds. However, if the deceased has a son, the daughter(s) are made agnatic heirs.

The *paternal grandfather* is entirely excluded from inheritance by the father or nearer paternal grandfather of the deceased. However, if they are not living, he takes their place, receiving one-sixth of the estate, or if there are no children of the deceased or the deceased's son h.l.s., he becomes an agnatic heir.

The *maternal grandmother* is entirely excluded by the living mother of the deceased or nearer maternal or paternal grandmother. The *paternal grandmother* is excluded by the living mother or father of the deceased, a nearer maternal or paternal grandmother and a nearer paternal grandfather. However, when they are not excluded, they receive a share of one-sixth of the inheritance to be distributed to one or to two or more collectively.

The *son's daughter* receives a share of one-half for one and two-thirds for two or more collectively. However, she is excluded from inheritance by the existence of the son or more than one daughter, or a higher son's daughter. If only one daughter of the deceased exists or if only one higher son's daughter exists, her share is reduced to one-sixth. Finally, if an equal son's son exists, she is made an agnatic heir.

The *full sister* of the deceased is excluded from inheritance by the deceased's son or son h.l.s., father, and paternal grandfather. If these are not living, one sister receives one-half of the estate and two or more collectively receive two-thirds. However, if a full brother exists, the full sister is made an agnatic heir.

The *consanguine sister* is excluded from inheritance by a son h.l.s., father, paternal grandfather, full brother, or more than one full sister. Otherwise her share is one-half for one sister and two-thirds collectively for two or more. When only one full sister exists, the consanguine sister's share is reduced to one-sixth and if a consanguine brother exists, the consanguine sister is made an agnatic heir.

The *uterine brother* and *uterine sister* are excluded by the child, child of a son h.l.s., father, or paternal grandfather of the deceased. If these do not exist, the uterine brother and/or sister receive one-sixth singly and one-third for two or more collectively.[18]

Agnatic Heirs

Once the *Quranic* heirs have received their share, the estate passes on to the Class II agnatic heirs *(asabah)*, or male relations on the male line. The inheritance rights of the agnates derive from pre-Islamic customary law.

Class II heirs have often been referred to as "residuaries" since the residue of the estate (often the bulk of the inheritance) goes to them. Class II contains all of the male agnates, and due to *Quranic* reforms, four specific female agnates.

Agnatic heirs are formally classified by the *Sirajiyyah*[19] in the following way:

1. Males — The agnate in his own right *(asabah bi-nafsihi)*. This group, the largest and most important, includes a limitless number of blood relatives, all male agnates who were the tribal heirs of pre-Islamic law—the son, son's son, father, brother, paternal uncle and his son, and so on.

2. Females—The agnate in the right of another *(asabah bi-ghayriha)*. This section specifies four female agnates *when they co-exist with male relatives of the same degree:* daughter (with son), son's daughter h.l.s. (with equal son's son h.l.s.), full sister (with full brother) and consanguine sister (with consanguine brother).

3. Females—the agnate with another *(asabah maa ghayriha)*. These consist of two irregular cases of full and consanguine sisters when they co-exist with daughters and there are no nearer heirs.[20]

Uterine Heirs

Following distribution to the *Quranic* and agnatic heirs, the inheritance that remains is distributed among the uterine heirs *(dhawu al-arham)*, often referred to as "distant kinsmen." Uterine heirs include every relative who is neither a sharer nor a residuary. On close examination, one finds that the agnatic and the uterine together include all possible blood relatives of the deceased.

Following the first three principal categories of heirs described above, the following four subsidiary classes of heirs (successors unrelated by blood) inherit only as a rare exception:

Successor by Contract

In Hanafi law, in default of all blood relations and subject to the rights of husband or wife, the estate of the deceased goes to the "successor by contract." Through a contract this person promises to pay a fine or ransom for which the deceased may become liable, and in exchange he receives this right of succession. Such an agreement is called a *mawalat*.

Acknowledged Kinsman

The next in succession is a person of unknown descent about whom the deceased has made an acknowledgement of kinship, not through himself but through another. The deceased could have acknowledged someone as his brother, the descendant of his father or his uncle, or the descendant of his grandfather, but not as his son.

Universal Legatee

The universal legatee is the person to whom the deceased, through a will, has left all of his property. The deceased may leave the whole estate if he has no living heir.

Escheat

In the default of all possible heirs mentioned above, the estate escheats to the government, the ultimate heir. In early Islamic history the inheritance would go to the Public Treasury (*bayt al-mal*).

Testamentary Bequests (wasiyyah)

As the Hanafi inheritance laws so fully reveal, a man is not free to bequeath his whole estate to whomever he chooses. He is obligated by law to give certain fixed amounts to specific heirs. These shares represent the inviolate right of such heirs to an inheritance.

However, the verses of inheritance had been preceded by earlier verses permitting testamentary bequests to relatives. The law of testamentary bequests has its source in the *Quran:* "It is prescribed when death approaches any of you, if he leave any goods, that he make a bequest to parents and next of kin, according to reasonable usage; this is due from the God-fearing"[21] (II:180). This *Quranic* "Verse of Bequests" which was of a general and discretionary nature has generally been regarded by the majority of jurists as abrogated by the later *Quranic* verses of inheritance which, as has been noted above, stipulated fixed portions for specified heirs. However, as will be seen in Chapter 3, a minority of jurists continued to maintain that the "Verse of Bequests" was in force. Modern Egyptian reforms have been based on this position.[22]

Since the *Quranic* verses of inheritance only provided for a specific group of heirs and this only "after payment of legacies and debts," some form of bequest was still presumed (IV:12). Because the *Quran* was silent as to the extent of this continued power of testamentary disposition, jurists turned to the *Sunnah* of the Prophet for regulations which both enabled bequests and protected the rights of *Quranic* heirs. The result is a system which recognizes the right of a Muslim to bequeath up to one-third of his net estate to parties of his own choice as long as they are not his own legal heirs. The bequest can be made for any person capable of owning property, regardless of his religion, or to an institution, or for a religious or charitable object.

The provision limiting the disposition of property to the "bequeathable third" is based on a report by the Companion of the Prophet, Saad b. Abi Waqqas:

> The Messenger of God visited me at Mecca... since I was near death. So I said to him: "My illness has become very serious. I-

have a good deal of property and my daughter is my only heir. Shall I give away all my property as alms?" He said: "No." I said: "Shall I bequeath two-thirds of my property as alms?" He said: "No." I asked: "Half?" He answered again: "No." Then he said: "Make a will for one-third and one-third is a great deal. It is better to leave your heirs rich than poor and begging from other people."[23]

The second restriction that a bequest may not be made in favor of a legal heir stems from the *hadith* reported by Ibn Abbas: "No legacy to an heir unless the other heirs agree."[24]

Sunni jurists, moreover, devised a further regulation to cover cases in which a testator went beyond the limits of his power and bequeathed in excess of the allowable one-third or bequeathed to an heir. In such cases, the permission of the testator's heirs is required before such provisions can take effect. In Hanafi law this consent must be obtained after the death of the testator.

Waqf (Charitable Endowment)

The legal definition of *waqf*, or endowment, in the Hanafi schools is "the detention of a specific thing in the ownership of the *waqif* or appropriator and the devoting or appropriating of its profits or usufruct in charity on the poor or other good objects."[25]

The formation of *waqfs* is consistent with the strong emphasis on charitable deeds that is stressed in Islam, but in comparison with other institutions, its support in traditions is weak. The legal scholars *(fuqaha)*, in explaining *waqf*, put most emphasis on a tradition of Ibn Umar which says that Umar asked the Prophet what he should do with valuable lands he had just acquired after the partition of Khaibar. The Prophet answered: "Retain the thing itself and devote its fruits to pious purposes." Umar followed these instructions, prohibiting the land from being sold, given away, or bequeathed and giving it as charity to the poor, needy relatives, slaves, wanderers, guests, and for the propagation of the faith. In addition, the property's maintainer could also obtain sustenance for the property as long as he did not accumulate wealth from it.

Certain conditions must be met for the completion of a

valid *waqf.* First of all, the founder of a *waqf (waqif)* must have reached puberty, be of sound mind and be a free man. He must also possess unrestricted ownership and full right of disposal of his property. Secondly, the object of the endowment must be of a permanent nature and it must yield a usufruct (profit). A *waqf* is generally associated with real estate although movable property has also been awarded. Thirdly, the *waqf* must be made in perpetuity *(muabbad)* so that if it is established for individuals, the proceeds are allotted after their death to the poor. Fourthly, the purpose of the *waqf* must be pleasing to God. In addition, the ultimate purpose of a *waqf* must be *qurbah* (i.e., for the benefit of the poor).

Two kinds of *waqf* can be distinguished: a religious or charitable endowment *(waqf khairi)* involving mosques, hospitals, bridges, etc., or family endowments *(waqf ahli* or *dhurri)* for children or grandchildren as well as other relatives or other people.

Only in Hanafi law can the *waqif* himself also benefit from the *waqf* after the dedication. For the remainder of his life or for a shorter period of time, he can take the whole of the usufruct from the *waqf.*

Waqfs can be made for the rich and the poor alike, or the rich and thereafter for the poor, or for the poor only. Thus, when a *waqf* is given in favor of the *waqif's* descendants, the trust is in their favor as long as a single descendant exists. When they cease to exist, the usufruct will go to the poor. Some limitation is placed on the amount of the *waqif's* estate dedicated in certain circumstances. If a *waqf* is made through a will or during death illness *(marad al-maut),* the testator cannot award more than one-third of his estate without the consent of his heirs.

CONCLUSION

The study of classical family law demonstrates the practical bent of Islam, from its earliest days, in applying the divine imperative. The comprehensiveness of the early Muslim jurists' efforts is attested to by the highly-developed and detailed regulations governing every aspect of marriage, divorce, and succession. As we have seen, these regulations embodied both *Quranic* reforms and customary legal practices.

Quranic reforms corrected many injustices in pre-Islamic society by granting women rights to which they were entitled—the right to contract their marriage, receive dower, retain possession and control of wealth, and receive maintenance and shares in inheritance. At the same time, however, family laws were formulated to meet a woman's needs in a society where her largely domestic, childbearing roles rendered her sheltered and dependent upon her father, her husband, and her close male relations. Thus, family law reflected woman's dependent position as can be seen in regulations concerning witnesses, option of puberty, initiation of divorce, and rights of maintenance and inheritance.

Since men had more independence, wider social contacts, and higher status in the world, their social position was translated into greater legal responsibilities (especially in maintenance regulations), as well as more extensive legal privileges proportionate to those responsibilities. The most notable examples of such rights and duties can be found in the areas of guardianship of marriage, extensive divorce rights, wider privileges of custody, and greater shares in inheritance.

In its attempts to meet the needs of a particular social milieu, Muslim family law reflected the social mores of the time— the traditional roles of men and women and the function of the extended family in a patriarchal society. This understanding of classical family law, which demonstrates the interrelatedness of law and society, provides a valuable perspective for modern legal reform. The duties and responsibilities of men and women in classical law remained virtually unchallenged up to the twentieth century because they paralleled the socially accepted roles of individuals and the function of the family in a basically unchanging society. Profound social forces in modern times have affected the status and roles of women and the family in Muslim society. This process has been accompanied by reforms in Muslim family law which have sought to respond to as well as to foster social change.

3

MODERN MUSLIM FAMILY LAW
REFORM IN EGYPT AND PAKISTAN

LEGAL REFORM IN EGYPT

Reform in the Ottoman Empire

N THE MIDDLE OF THE NINETEENTH CENTURY, reform in the Middle East was initiated in the Ottoman Empire, of which Egypt was a part, through the promulgation of commercial and penal codes.[1] These codes, both in form and substance, were largely derived from European codes as a result of increasingly close contact with the West (especially France and Great Britain) in the nineteenth century. In addition, secular *(Nizamiyyah)* courts were established to handle civil and criminal law, and so the jurisdiction of the *Shariah* courts was limited to the area of family law.

The above legal reforms were at first followed by Egypt as an Ottoman province, but in 1874 Egypt gained judicial and administrative independence. Nevertheless, foreign legal influence prevailed, and so from 1875 onwards the Egyptian government enacted civil and criminal codes modeled on French law.

Islamic law was still central to family law, however. In 1875 Muhammad Qadri Pasha, under official government sponsorship, compiled a code based on the classical Hanafi school which included 647 articles concerning family law inheritance.[2]

Although this code was never officially adopted as legislation, as a compendium of classical law it was used as the major reference for Egyptian *Shariah* courts and for the courts of other Middle Eastern countries as well.

Despite all the official legal change in the areas of civil and criminal law during the latter half of the nineteenth century, Muslim family law, which had been practiced through the centuries, remained unchanged. The fact that no major legislation in family law occurred until 1920 was consistent with the lack of social progress in Egypt.

Egyptian Reformers

The ills of a medieval society in a modernizing world had been identified and criticized and the seeds for legal reform in Egypt planted by such important figures as Rifaah Badawi Rafi al-Tahtawi, Muhammad Abduh, and Qasim Amin, who attempted to provide a Muslim rationale for change. Tahtawi, the most significant figure of the first half of the nineteenth century, emphasized the necessity and legitimacy of adapting Islamic law to new social circumstances. He recommended using the principle of *takhayyur*, an accepted method of jurisprudence according to which a Muslim in a specific situation was permitted to go outside his own school of law and follow the interpretation of one of the other Sunni schools. This suggestion was adopted and used extensively by later modernists.

It was left to the next generation and Muhammad Abduh, often called the "Father of Muslim Modernism," to grapple with the reality of change and to articulate an Islamic rationale for reform. Recognizing the discrepancy between *Quranic* reforms and women's social status in the nineteenth century, Abduh criticized the waywardness of Muslim society: "The Muslims have erred in the education and training of women, and in not teaching them about their rights; and we have failed to follow the guidance of our religion, becoming an argument against it."[3]

Abduh was especially critical of polygamy and its deleterious effect on family life. The *Quranic* argument that Abduh developed regarding polygamy was to be adopted by all modernist reformers as will be shown. For Abduh, polygamy had been permitted in the Prophet's time as a concession to the prevailing social conditions. However, the true intent of the *Quran*, its ideal, was monogamy. *Quranic* texts (IV:3 and IV:129) establish the norm that more than one wife was only permissible when equal justice and impartiality were guaranteed. Since this is a practical impossibility, Abduh concluded that the *Quranic* ideal must be monogamy.[4]

While Abduh remained principally concerned with theological and legal reform, his associate, Qasim Amin, developed the social dimension of the modernist movement by focusing on the plight of Muslim women as a cause for the deterioration of the family and society. Amin was especially critical of arranged marriages, the wife's lack of power to divorce, and the husband's unlimited rights of divorce, all of which he believed perpetuated the bondage of women.

Following Abduh, Amin re-emphasized the original *Quranic* intent that divorce be viewed as reprehensible, although permissible when necessitated by failure of the marriage and of attempts at arbitration. As a step toward providing some relief, he recommended that women have equal rights of divorce with men.[5]

Reactions to Amin's feminist books, *Tahrir al-Marah* (The Emancipation of Women) and *al-Marah al-jadidah* (The New Woman), and to his ideas were swift and harshly critical. However, his writings became a source of inspiration to many feminists. Madame Huda Shaarawi, leader of the Feminist Movement in Egypt a generation later, hailed him as "the hero of the feminist awakening and its founder."[6]

Modern Family Law Reform in Egypt

In the midst of this social ferment, initial legal efforts for reform of law were made first in the Ottoman Empire and later in Egypt itself. The beginnings of reform in the twentieth century were slow both because of the stagnant social situation and the political problems caused by Western intervention and World War I. Significant reform legislation did not occur in Egypt until 1920. But from this time on, Egyptian jurisprudence and legislation was to provide the impetus for modernist legislation throughout the Arab world.

Reform in family law occurred in the following areas: marriage, divorce, inheritance, and religious endowments.

Marriage

In 1897 the *Egyptian Code of Organization and Procedure for Shariah Courts* required written documentation in marriage, divorce, and certain inheritance claims. The traditional oral contract through which evidence was limited to oral (and thus often hearsay) evidence had presented many legal difficulties: false claims of marriage and denial of valid marriages, problems which in an increasingly mobile society undermined the institution of marriage and the family.

The importance of documentation was further delineated in the *Code of 1909–1910* as amended in 1913, which decreed that after 1911 all legal claims must rely on "official certificates" or documents written and signed by the deceased.[7] This requirement of official documentation was also utilized in dealing with a more specific social problem, child marriage. In 1923, registrars of marriage were instructed not to conclude marriages or register and issue official certificates of marriage for brides less than sixteen and grooms less than eighteen. Eight years later, the *Law of the Organization and Procedure of Shariah Courts of 1931* consolidated the above provision with the regulation that henceforth courts were prohibited from hearing claims of disputed marriages unless these marriages could be established by an official certificate. In addition, the courts were prohibited from hearing any claims in cases in which the bride and groom had not reached the minimum age at the time of the claim (*Article 99*).

By refusing to register child marriages and by denying such marriages judicial relief, the reforms severely limited child marriages indirectly. Direct intervention, the declaring of child marriages as invalid, would have been considered an act of *ijtihad* (interpretation) which would have made passage of the law virtually impossible. The indirect means was justified on the basis of the *siyasah shariyyah* doctrine, the right of a ruler to take administrative steps where necessary to insure a society ruled by the *Shariah.*

Divorce

As the *Quran's* primary legislative concern was the improvement of women's status through the establishment and protection of her rights, so too the main motivation behind modern Egyptian family law reform was the uplifting of women's position. Divorce was the area most in need of reform. Modern legislation sought first to establish grounds that would enable women to sue for judicial divorce, and second to limit a husband's exercise of repudiation *(talaq).*

In the Hanafi school, the authoritative school for Egyptian *Shariah* courts, there are virtually no grounds by which a wife can free herself from an undesirable marriage except for her husband's impotence[8] or by exercising the "option of puberty."[9] Of the four schools of law (Hanafi, Maliki, Shafii, Hanbali) the Hanafi school is the most rigidly formalistic since it was more concerned with the development of a logical legal mechanism than with intention. Unlike wives in the non-Hanafi schools, and especially the Maliki school, which was the most liberal in this regard, wives under Hanafi law had to endure desertion and maltreatment with no recourse through divorce.

The first changes in the laws of divorce occurred in the Ottoman Empire in 1915 with the promulgation of two imperial edicts *(Iradah)* granting women the right to sue for divorce in cases of desertion or the existence of a husband's contagious disease making conjugal life dangerous (venereal disease, leprosy, etc.). More importantly, these edicts were soon followed in 1917 by the *Ottoman Law of Family Rights* which constituted the first officially adopted codification of Muslim family law in the modern period.

In Egypt, broader grounds for divorce were established by *Law No. 25 of 1920* and *Law No. 25 of 1929.* This reform legislation recognized four situations in which a woman could sue for divorce: (1) her husband's failure to provide maintenance *(nafaqah);* (2) dangerous or contagious disease of the husband; (3)

desertion; and (4) maltreatment. The juristic basis for this change was the doctrine of *takhayyur* or "selection" suggested previously by Tahtawi as a means for reform—the ability of an individual to go outside his own personal school of law and select a resolution to a specific problem from the remaining three Sunni schools. The legislators now used this principle in departing from Hanafi law and adopting the more liberal and equitable teaching of the Maliki school.

Islamic law had granted every wife the right to support or maintenance. However, the prevailing Hanafi opinion had caused great inequity since the husband's responsibility for maintenance only specified present maintenance, and not past-due maintenance that he had not provided, unless a distinct agreement concerning this was previously made.[10] Thus, even in the most extreme cases of non-support, a wife lacked the right to sue for divorce. Prior to the passing of reform legislation, the maximum punitive measure for failure to pay maintenance was imprisonment.

To remedy this situation, *Article 1* of the *Law of 1920* decreed that maintenance was a cumulative debt owed by the husband to his wife, commencing with the first time the husband failed to support his wife.[11] The situation of a divorced wife was declared to be similar; *Article 2* stipulated her maintenance debt should be computed from the date of her divorce.

In non-support cases, *Articles 4 and 5* decreed that a wife could obtain a decree of maintenance which could then be executed from any of her husband's property. This stipulation differed from classical Hanafi law in which maintenance could only be executed out of property similar in nature to the required maintenance (i.e., clothes, furniture, food, money, etc.).

However, the most significant legal innovation occurred in *Article 4* which decreed that non-support due to a husband's incapacity or unwillingness to support constitutes grounds for a wife's divorce suit. The only exception permitted involved cases of destitution in which the husband was granted a grace period of not more than one month.

If the husband is absent or imprisoned and if there is a lack of property from which his wife's maintenance can be extracted, the wife is then also entitled to a divorce on grounds of non-support. If, on the other hand, the husband is at a great distance or if his location is unknown, the wife is granted a divorce at once (*Article 5*).

The key factor in maintenance cases is the willingness and capacity of the husband to support his wife. Practically speaking, he is given a further period to prove himself—the *iddah* (waiting) period. A judicial divorce granted in non-support cases is revocable, and payment of the current maintenance is proof of good will and sufficient to revoke the divorce. However, unlike Hanafi law, under the new legislation the husband still remains responsible for past maintenance as a debt owed to his wife.

Although most of the modern reforms in Muslim family law were motivated by desires to better the lot of women, certain safeguards were also introduced to protect the husband from legal abuses with respect to maintenance and the maximum length of *iddah*. Hanafi law stipulated that should a woman cease to menstruate before the end of her *iddah* she was to receive maintenance until the completion of three menses *(quru)* or until she reached menopause, whichever came first. Of course, such measures were intended to continue to maintain the woman who may be pregnant. However, since the amount of time for completion of three menses was dependent upon the woman's testimony alone, many abuses were possible and so some women did claim maintenance for very extended periods of time.

The reform of this situation was achieved in two phases— the first in 1920 and the second in 1929. Using *takhayyur* and following *Maliki* law again, *Article 3* of *Law No. 25 of 1920* stated that *iddah* for maintenance ended if after nursing her infant (usually for a period of two years) the woman did not have a menses for a complete year (twelve consecutive months). The effect was to fix definite limits (both minimum and maximum in cases where pregnancy was possible). Even if a woman were to lie about completing three menses, the fixing of a twelve-month limit meant the maximum *iddah* possible was three years without nursing and five years with, instead of the previously indefinite duration.

In the 1929 reform the rules of maintenance for wives observing *iddah* was carried one step further. While the legislation of 1920 had set minimum and maximum periods for the *iddah*, yet injustices were still possible since women could claim observance of *iddah* for a maximum of three to five years. Complaints of such injustices were cited as the cause for the new regulation. Based on modern medical expertise, the maximum length of *iddah* was set at one year from the date of divorce. This regulation was applied in cases of maintenance, as well as inheritance and paternity.[12]

Related to the question of maintenance is the custody (*hadanah*) of children.[13] Claiming to respond to complaints of mothers that their children were removed from their custody at too early an age (seven for boys and nine for girls), the *Law of 1929* decreed that when in the judgment of the court it seemed beneficial, the court would extend maternal custody of children to nine years for boys and eleven years for girls. (*Article 7*). Because in this instance the court chose to stay within the Hanafi school, reforms were minimal. They failed to consider the psychological hardship to the mother. The criterion of the Hanafi school was that the custody of children pass from the mother to the father when the boy no longer needed a woman's services and when the girl had reached the age of desire. In fact, the majority view had set these ages at seven and nine respectively, but the court chose to follow the minority of jurists who preferred nine and eleven.

The third and fourth grounds giving a woman the right to sue for divorce, maltreatment and desertion, were established through the *Law No. 25 of 1929*. Maltreatment or cruelty (*darar*) finds its only support as a ground for divorce in the *Maliki* school.[14] Following this source, *Article 6* decreed that where a wife's allegation of maltreatment detrimental to the continued marital relationship is substantiated and reconciliation seems impossible, the *qadi* shall grant the wife an irrevocable divorce.

Furthermore, the law granted the wife the right to re-petition the *qadi* if her first petition is denied on grounds of unsubstantiated evidence. In the event of a second rejection of her petition, the *qadi* is required to appoint two arbitrators for the partners. Following the *Quranic* injunction "If ye fear a breach between them twain, Appoint (two) arbiters, One from his family, and the other from hers," (IV:35) each assigned arbitrator should represent one of the spouses. If this is not possible, men acquainted with the circumstances of the case should be appointed (*Article 7*). Their task is a thorough investigation of the causes for the marital conflict and the submission of recommendations to the court for a reconciliation *(Article 8)*. If reconciliation proves impossible, and if responsibility for the conflict lies with the husband, with both spouses, or if the source of the conflict is unknown, the *qadi* is instructed to grant a single but irrevocable divorce.[15]

The above concerns for justice and possible reconciliation were further underscored by *Articles 10 and 11*. *Article 10* stipulates that should the report of the arbitrators indicate a deadlock, the *qadi* is to order them to make a fresh attempt. Should their renewed efforts prove fruitless, then other arbitrators are to be appointed. And finally, the court is to render its judgment in accordance with the recommendation of the arbitrators' report *(Article 11)*. Thus, through detailed procedures, every attempt is made to insure a just and equitable decision.

The fourth and final ground for divorce is desertion. Hanafi law was particularly rigid regarding desertion. The only relief available to a wife occurred if her husband was missing for a period of ninety years from the date of his birth.[16] This was believed to constitute a reasonable amount of time after which the husband might be presumed dead. After the expiration of this period, the court would declare his wife a putative widow.

In response to this problem, the legislation of 1929 decreed that if a husband was absent for one year or more without sufficient reason,[17] a wife had the right to sue for an irrevocable divorce on the grounds of injury due to his unwarranted absence. If the husband can be reached, the *qadi* must inform him of the pending suit. The husband's failure to return or make arrangements for his wife to join him will result in a decree of divorce. If, on the other hand, contact with the husband proves impossible, the court must then grant the wife a divorce immediately *(Article 13)*. Moreover, a petition based on desertion may be initiated even if the husband has property from which the wife's maintenance can be obtained *(Article 12)*. Thus, the importance of conjugal life was upheld as central to the marriage contract and payment of support was not allowed to substitute for the husband's presence.

Article 14 of the *Law of 1929* addressed itself to a specific kind of desertion which had been the source of much hardship, the husband's imprisonment. In an increasingly modernized society in

which virtually all punishment for crimes resulted in imprisonment, the plight of convicts' wives, who were unable to free
themselves from marriages that were financially and psychologi-
cally undesirable, became a controversial issue in the press. As a
remedy, the law decreed that a woman whose husband had been
sentenced to not less than three years may, after a separation of at
least one year, petition the court for divorce.

The second major reform of Muslim family law in Egypt
was the limitation of the husband's unilateral power to divorce his
wife at his own discretion at any time and for any reason. The
Quranic injunctions regarding just and equitable treatment of
wives had been morally but not legally binding. Hanafi law, with
its emphasis on form rather than intention, further complicated
and contributed to injustice since a divorce uttered by the husband under compulsion, intoxication, or jest was held to be valid
regardless of the intention of the husband.[18] Reformers sought to
limit and correct this situation in *Egyptian Law No. 25, 1929.*

Article 1 decreed that all formulae of divorce uttered
under compulsion or in a state of intoxication were henceforth
invalid. Metaphorical statements with ambiguous meanings were
also declared to be invalid unless divorce was actually intended.[19]
This emphasis on intention found its sources and hence justification in the Maliki and Shafii rather than the Hanafi school.

From a juristic point of view, the more radical reforms
occurred in *Articles 2* and *3* since their contents lacked any basis in
the official (predominant) views of the four Sunni schools. Instead,
individual jurists such as Ibn Taymiyah were cited as sources. This
extension of *takhayyur* to the selection of an individual jurist as the
authoritative source for a reform represented a new expansion of
the principle.

The main problem faced by *Article 2* was conditional
expressions of divorce pronounced by the husband either as a
threat against his wife (or third party) or as an oath to reinforce a
statement. Again the effect of such pronouncements was made
contingent upon intention and not mere uttering of formulae.
Thus the law stipulates that all such conditional utterances effect
a divorce only if the husband really intended to dissolve his
marriage.

An even more significant departure from traditional practice was the decree that regardless of the number of times indicated by word or sign, a pronouncement of divorce shall only be considered as single and revocable *(Article 3)*. Thus, the practice of *talaq al-bidah* (the three declarations of divorce given at one time) which, although frowned upon, had nevertheless been recognized as valid by classical law, was finally rendered ineffective.[20]

The *talaq al-bidah* had resulted in many abuses of *Quranic* regulations. First, it bypassed the waiting period *(iddah)* which the *Quran* had intended for reconciliation. Furthermore, since this divorce was irrevocable, remarriage was impossible without an intervening marriage of the wife to another man. Among the practices that resulted was that of *tahlil* (making lawful). Its aim was the circumvention of the impediment to remarriage resulting from a triple repudiation. The former (divorced) husband would arrange the marriage of his former wife to another man *(muhallil)* with the understanding that upon consummation (real or pretended) the second man would then divorce her. Only then would the former husband and wife be free to remarry.[21]

The reforms of 1920 and 1929 did not include all the areas in the laws of marriage and divorce recognized to be in need of reform. In 1926 the Egyptian government appointed a committee to recommend reforms in Islamic law governing marriage and divorce. Influenced by the reformist spirit of Muhammad Abduh, suggestions contained in the draft articles submitted were: first, (following Hanbali teaching) that wives be permitted to include stipulations in their marriage contracts provided that they were not contrary to the purposes of marriage. For example, a marriage contract may include the provision that the husband may not marry a second wife. Second, that a man should be restricted from taking a second wife and that officials be prohibited from registering such a marriage contract without permission of the local *qadi*. Third, that the *qadi* should be required to investigate petitions for a second marriage to determine whether the man was capable of equal treatment and support of a second wife as well as his present wife and family.

The *Explanatory Memorandum* which accompanied the above draft articles is especially instructive for it contained not only juristic bases for the reforms, but also references to the contemporary Egyptian social situation to justify its suggestions. Regarding the inclusion of stipulations in a marriage contract, the *Memorandum* noted that oral promises are often made by prospective husbands but ignored after the marriage, a situation that leaves wives without written legal evidence through which they can cite their grievances and seek judicial relief. The argument for the draft articles concerned with restrictions on polygamy noted that the vast majority of neglected children in Egypt were the result of polygamous marriages contracted by men who were incapable of supporting even one family.

The Egyptian Cabinet approved these draft articles. However, they caused such a controversy that King Fuad refused to support these proposals. As a result, they were not incorporated in *Law No. 25 of 1929.*

Similar recommendations were proposed by the Ministry of Social Affairs in 1943, 1945, and 1969. A major attempt at family law reform occurred again in 1971 when the drafting of a new constitution for Egypt raised the question of the role of the *Shariah* in the new constitution. Feminist leaders such as Dr. Latifah al-Zayatt and Mrs. Fatimah Abd al-Hamid called for a "new law of personal status" which would treat more effectively such major problems as polygamy, divorce, and custody of children.[22] Moreover, Dr. Aisha Ratib, a professor of law at Cairo University called for the imposition of restrictions on polygamy and the requirement that divorce be obtained from a judge.[23] In November of 1971 Dr. Ratib was named Minister of Social Affairs. The Committee for the Revision of Family Law, (headed by Dr. Ratib), made the following suggestions: (1) raising the age at which marriage is legally possible to 18 for girls and 21 for boys. (2) requiring permission of a judge for a polygamous marriage; (3) allowing divorces to take place only in the presence of a judge who would first attempt a reconciliation between husband and wife (if a husband pronounces his wife divorced, although his act would be valid according to Islamic *Shariah,* he would be punished by law); (4) stipulating that the mother's guardianship be extended to the age of 10 for boys and 12 for girls; or that her guardianship should last until "the coming of age" for the boy and until marriage for the girl; and that guardianship of children at any age should go to the most suitable of the parents.[24] (5) encouraging the "judge's specialization" to facilitate fair and competent handling of family law cases. (A number of judges exclusively concerned with "family law problems" would be provided so that each could devote sufficient time to study such cases and so that the judge could acquire a proper perspective in handling cases of divorce, alimony, etc. It was also suggested that cases involving family problems be handled by a female judge who would be more capable of understanding the particular position of the wife or children in family disagreements).

In addition, the Committee recommended that special halls be provided so that each divorce would be discussed privately, thus guaranteeing "secrecy and safety" to the family involved. This would counteract the traditional argument opposing the handling of divorce cases in court because it would expose private family problems to public view.[25]

Finally, in June 1979, Egypt enacted Law No. 44 which consisted of further family law amendments and contained a number of important provisions. First, a wife must be informed if her husband takes another wife, and she has the right to sue for divorce if she disapproves of the marriage (Art. 6b). Furthermore, if a husband conceals from his new wife that he is already married, this, too, will constitute grounds for divorce by the new wife (Art. 6b).

Second, the husband must obtain a notarized certificate of divorce, and he is obligated to inform his wife of the divorce (Art. 5b). This measure sought to remedy situations in which a man might repudiate, or claim to have repudiated, his wife without telling her, continue to live with her, but, at a later date, refuse maintenance for any children born during this period on the grounds of their illegitimacy. Furthermore, if a woman is divorced without her consent and without just cause, she is entitled to at least two years additional alimony in addition to maintenance during the *iddah* period.

The reform legislation provides a curious means for a woman to obtain a quick divorce. As noted previously, Egyptian family law included a provision known as *bayt al-taah* (house of obedience) which meant that a husband could restrict his wife to their home. Whereas under traditional Egyptian law, a wife who "refused to obey" and left her husband might be forcefully re-

turned by the police and confined until she became more obe-
dient, the reform law of 1979 decreed that if a wife refused to
return after her husband sent her formal notice through a bailiff,
the marriage is terminated from the date of refusal. Given the
husband's unfettered unilateral right of divorce, this reform seems
to be less for his protection than to free a wife from the constraints
of *bayt al-taah* and provide her with a quick, effective means of
divorce.

Where divorce occurs, a man must pay child support until
his daughters are married and until his sons reach fifteen years of
age or complete their education, whichever comes first (Art. 18c).
In addition, a divorced mother with custody of minor children may
be awarded the family apartment by the court until she remarries
or her custody of the children ceases, unless her former husband
provides another appropriate dwelling (Art. 4).

Third, the reform legislation raised the custody ages so
that a woman's right of custody terminates when the boy reaches
ten and the girl twelve years of age (Art. 20). Furthermore, the
courts are given greater discretion in custody cases. A judge may
now permit a mother to retain custody of her daughters until their
marriage and of her sons until they reach fifteen years of age if this
is considered in the best interest of the children (Art. 20).

The reform legislation also addresses the question of the
relationship of a woman's modern recognized right to work and her
traditionally sanctioned obligations as wife and mother. While
maintaining a woman's right to work, this right is a "conditioned
right," that is, it must not be incompatible with the interests of her
family (Art. 2). If it is and she refuses to heed her husband's request
that she refrain from work, she loses her right to his support.

With regard to the recent Egyptian reforms, several
points are noteworthy: First, in order to avoid the blocking of draft
legislation as had occurred in 1975, President Anwar Sadat followed an alternative means of effecting legislation. He exercised
his constitutional right to issue a presidential decree during a
parliamentary recess. Thus, all that remained was a simple vote of
confirmation by parliament when it convened. Second, as has
been true in most Muslim countries, penalties for noncompliance
with the new law were relatively light. Thus, for example, a man
who divorces his wife ignoring the procedures stipulated by this

law is liable to a maximum sentence of six months imprisonment and/or a maximum fine of 200 Egyptian pounds. Finally, despite these reforms, it remains ironic that Egypt, which was a leader in family law reform in the Middle East and continues to be a country in which women enjoy a relatively advanced status, still has not been able to pass legislation requiring that a husband obtain court permission for a polygamous marriage or a divorce.

Summary

As can be seen, the first Egyptian reforms in family law sought to improve the lot of Muslim women. A major concern of the *Quran* was marriage and the family, especially the safeguarding of the rights of wives. Thus, to preclude abuses that had crept into Muslim practice, reforms in marriage and divorce were introduced.

To prevent false marriage claims and especially to control the social problem of ill-conceived child marriages, official documentation of marriage transactions as well as the raising of minimum marriage ages was required.

To counter Muslim men's abuse of their right of repudiation *(talaq)*, reforms were introduced that restricted their exercise of *talaq*, expanded the grounds entitling women to a divorce, and improved women's custody and maintenance rights. Again, a return to the *Quran* is evident.

In addition to reforms in marriage and divorce, attention turned to other areas of family law which were also in need of reform: inheritance *(faraid*, the allotted portions), testamentary bequest *(wasiyyah)*, and religious endowment *(waqf)*.

Inheritance

Unlike the family law reforms of 1920 and 1929 which had been of an *ad hoc* nature and thus rather piecemeal, legislation in two of the three areas, inheritance and testamentary disposition, was drafted in systematic codes. The result was the *Law of Inheritance of 1943* and the *Law of Testamentary Dispositions of 1946*.

The thrust of the reforms reflected, as did the reforms in marriage and divorce, a desire to strengthen the rights of nuclear family members and to rectify injustices resulting from the application of certain rules from medieval textbooks that reflected and suited the extended family of traditional Islamic society, but no longer adequately met the needs of the modern world.

A prime example of the inequity caused by the misapplication of some traditional laws in modern society concerns the inheritance rights of collaterals (brothers and sisters) of the deceased. Hanafi law reflected the traditional family whose wealth maintained all other members in a large extended household. Therefore, collaterals of the deceased were completely excluded from inheriting by their father's father (paternal grandfather). The real injustice of this situation arose when, according to law, the deceased's wealth, which the grandfather had inherited, passed on to the deceased's uncle upon the death of the grandfather. In effect, then, the brothers and sisters of the deceased were excluded from inheritance by their uncle.

In order to strengthen the rights of nuclear family members, *Article 22* decreed that brothers and sisters were to enjoy the right of succession to the deceased's estate along with the grandfather.

A second important change introduced by the *Law of 1943* concerned the presumptions of law which determined the inheritance rights of a foetus. Although the general rule in all the schools was that the child must be born alive to inherit, Hanafi law admitted one exception, a child stillborn due to an assault on a pregnant woman. All four Sunni schools had held that the stillborn child of such an assault was entitled to a compensatory sum *(ghirrah)* paid by the perpetrator and passing to the heirs of the child. However, unlike the other schools, the Hanafi school extended this rule and concluded that the stillborn child had a general right of inheritance which then was passed on to his heirs.

Article 2 departed from the official teaching of all four schools, maintaining that the stillborn has no right to property, not even that of *ghirrah*. Rather, *ghirrah* was redefined as a payment to the mother to which she alone is entitled as compensation for the assault and her loss.

The more important and complex legal reform concerned

the determination of minimum and maximum periods of gestation. The vast majority of jurists had considered six months to be the minimum period of gestation for a married woman. Her child's right of inheritance, then, was contingent upon its birth within six months of her husband's death, on the grounds that a baby born after this period may well have been conceived after the husband's death.

Influenced by modern medical opinion and attempting to make the law reflect the normal course of nature, the *Egyptian Law of Inheritance* extended the minimum limit to 270 days based on a Hanbali opinion. A child born to a married woman within 270 days from the death of her spouse was considered to be the legitimate heir of the deceased *(Article 43)*.

On the other hand, the maximum gestation period which, under Hanafi law was two years for a revocable divorce and indefinite for an irrevocable divorce, enabled a widow to claim paternity for a child born more than a year after her husband's death — a medical impossibility. The inheritance rights thus claimed by the illegitimate child violated the rights of the real members of the nuclear family. *Article 43* also decreed that a child was entitled to full inheritance rights if he is born within a maximum of 365 days of his mother's separation *(furqah)* or widowhood.

Testamentary Bequests

Even more significant from the viewpoint of social and legal change is the *Law of Testamentary Dispositions of 1946*. Its two major reforms are: the acceptance of the principle of "Obligatory Bequests" and the recognition of a Muslim's right to make bequests to whomever he wishes.

Whereas the majority of Muslim jurists have held that the "Verses of Inheritance" *(faraid* verses) completely abrogated the "Verse of Bequests" (II:180), a small number of jurists (among them al-Shafii) maintained that this contention was only true of legal heirs who, under the "Verses of Inheritance," were entitled to a fixed share of inheritance. He maintained that it was praiseworthy *(mandub)* to make bequests to close relatives who were not heirs. Another jurist, Ibn Hazm, considered such be-

quests (to relatives who did not qualify as legal heirs) to be obligatory. Furthermore, other early jurists held that should the
deceased neglect this obligation, the court should make the obligatory bequest in his behalf.

Basing themselves on such traditional authorities, the
reformers further specified which relatives were to be entitled to
obligatory bequests.[26] The specific problem necessitating this
legislation involved the plight of orphaned grandchildren. Under
Islamic law and the principle of succession that the nearer in
degree excludes the more remote, orphaned grandchildren had no
legal claim to share in the estate of their deceased grandfather and
obtain that portion which would normally be due their predeceased parent if he were alive. Reformers were reluctant to
interfere with the law of succession since no basis could be found in
traditional authority for such an action.

In order to correct this injustice, *Article 76* stated that if a
grandfather failed to make a legacy to his orphaned grandchildren
in the amount to which their predeceased parent would have been
entitled by way of inheritance, the court shall execute such a
bequest from the estate of the deceased grandfather provided that
it does not exceed the one-third limitation.[27] Furthermore, all
such obligatory bequests are to take precedence over voluntary
bequests *(Article 78)*.

Article 37 introduced a change of far-reaching social consequences and one which departed sharply from the classical texts.
Following the Prophet's alleged statement, "No bequest in favor of
an heir," the general rule of all four Sunni schools was that bequests were restricted to non-heirs. Bequests in favor of an heir
required the ratification of the remaining heirs.

In a major departure from classical Hanafi law, however,
the *Law of Testamentary Bequests* decreed that a bequest to an
heir not exceeding one-third of the estate is valid and effective
regardless of the consent of the other heirs. A testator is now free
to will up to a third of his estate to heirs and non-heirs alike. Such a
change makes the Islamic legal system more responsive to individual circumstances. Previously, relatives who were wealthy or
poor, loving or hateful, had been treated alike. One special problem remedied by allowing bequests to be awarded to heirs involved the widow who received a very inadequate share. Her

largest inheritance had amounted to one-fourth of the estate; however, if she had surviving children, her share was reduced to one-eighth, an amount she may have had to divide with other wives in the case of a polygamous union.

The motive behind this reform legislation, as with most of the family law reform, was the strengthening of the rights of nuclear family members, as opposed to those of agnates in the extended tribal family. This could also alleviate the unreasonable situation in which a man with a daughter and a distant agnate relative (that he might not know or might actually dislike) would be forced to award the agnate one-half of his estate.

Religious Endowment (Waqf)

The last piece of major modernist reform legislation enacted by the Egyptian government during this period was the *Law of Rules Relevant to Waqf of 1946*. Like the *Law of Inheritance of 1943* and the *Law of Testamentary Dispositions of 1946*, this new legislation was the product of the Committee of Personal Status which had been established in 1936. The change introduced by *Article 1* of the *Law of Waqf of 1946* developed from the *Egyptian Code of Procedure for Shariah Courts, 1897* discussed earlier in this chapter.[28] The 1897 law had introduced the requirement of documentation to avoid the difficulties which often arose with oral testimony. The scope of this law had covered not only marriage but *waqf* claims as well by stipulating that the creation of a *waqf* must be accompanied by a document of declaration *(ishhad)*. Reform had been effected indirectly by forbidding judicial relief where the document was lacking.[29]

Subsequently, *Article 1* of the law of 1946 took the direct step of requiring that in the creation, alteration and revocation of a *waqf*, a declaration must be made before the *Shariah* courts and registered as well.

In addition, the law of 1946 also touched upon more substantial concerns related to the family. The law itself was in no way comprehensive. Rather, the purpose of its 62 articles was to bring the law of *waqf* (pious foundation, religious endowment) into line with those of inheritance and bequests and thus correct two major abuses which had occasioned widespread criticism: (1) the *waqf* system had immobilized considerable amounts of land and thus caused its withdrawal from agricultural and commercial use (especially industrial development); and (2) many had used the *waqf* system to bypass the laws of inheritance by excluding a particular heir or by including those not entitled to inherit. Women, especially daughters of the founder of a *waqf*, were victims of this discrimination. Fathers would try to avoid giving married daughters their fixed *Quranic* shares since it might break up the family estate.

A common practice employed to bypass women's inheritance rights was the inclusion of stipulations which, if not adhered to, voided the beneficiary's right to income from the *waqf*. For example, a father would specify that upon marriage, his daughter would lose her share. *Article 6* corrected this injustice by decreeing that a *waqf* that was joined with a condition restricting freedom as regards a marriage or place of residence was valid, but that the condition was null and void. Thus, conditions contrary to the spirit of the *Shariah* would no longer be enforced by the courts.

A major departure from the traditional law under which all *waqfs* had been perpetual was the declaration in *Article 5* that all family *waqfs* must be temporary, not extending to more than two generations (sixty years) or two series of beneficiaries. Even public *waqfs* under the new law (except for mosques and cemeteries which are necessarily perpetual) may also be temporary. The temporary nature of *waqf* was further established by *Article 11* under which the founder of a *waqf* created subsequent to this law was given the right of revocation. The rigidity of the *waqf* system was eliminated.

The purpose of this regulation was also to limit the effects of circumvention of the laws of inheritance by the founder of a *waqf*. Under the traditional system of perpetual family *waqfs*, discrimination had affected not only the disinherited legal heir but also all descendants *in perpetuo* whose needs and merits were unknown to the founder.[30] Among the principal beneficiaries of this regulation were the descendants of disenfranchised daughters.

The termination of a temporary *waqf* had raised much

controversy in Egypt. *Article 16,* which had prescribed that a temporary *waqf* would end upon the death of the beneficiaries or the expiration of a certain period of time, raised the question of what would happen to the property no longer subject to *waqf.* The predominant opinion of the Hanafi school stated that the ownership belonged to God. The reformers, however, looked to the other schools for a resolution. The Maliki school maintained that ownership remained with the founder, while the Hanbali school taught that ownership passed to the founder's beneficiaries. The resolution was not the product of one school, but rather of both. The Egyptian law applied the Maliki rule in cases where the founder was alive and the Hanbali rule when the founder was dead *(Article 17).*

The method used to provide authoritative support for this change is known as *talfiq* (patching together). *Talfiq* is a method by which the views of different schools or jurists are combined to form a single regulation.

Perhaps the most significant reforms in terms of the family occurred in *Articles 23–30* which provided for "obligatory entitlements" for the immediate family. Paralleling *Article 37* of the *Law of Testamentary Dispositions, Article 23* extended the right of a property owner to create a *waqf* not exceeding one-third of his estate in favor of whomever he desires, heir as well as non-heir or charity.

This provision, like its parallel in the *Law of Testamentary Dispositions,* enables a man to make extra provision for the needs of a member or members of his immediate family such as his wife and/or daughters. In addition to their rightful inheritance as heirs under the law of succession, the usufruct of up to one-third of the estate might be diverted from more distant agnatic residuaries to members of the immediate family. It should also be noted that this legislation concerns the rights of descendants and the parents, spouse (or spouses) of the deceased, and not grandparents or collaterals. These articles reflect the shift from an emphasis on the extended family to the nuclear family and the individual. The obligation of family members for more distant relatives, as social mobility separates extended family members, was lessened in law.

Two further provisions insure priority of the immediate family. First, the law stipulates that should the owner of property wish to endow all of his property, such a *waqf* must be in favor of such descendants as are alive at his death. Only if none of them are alive can he make a *waqf* to whomever he pleases. Second, *Article 24* decreed that in all *waqfs* which comprised more than one-third of the deceased founder's property, the descendants, parents, and spouse (or spouses) had a right to an entitlement. This obligatory entitlement amounts to the equivalent of their "fixed shares" *(faraid)* under their *Quranic* rights of inheritance whether or not they were named beneficiaries of the *waqf*. Furthermore, this entitlement devolves upon their deaths to their descendants.

The effect of *Articles 23 and 24* was to make two-thirds of the founder's estate subject to the rights of inheritance and to prevent the circumvention of these rights by a false use of *waqf*.

The general tendency of the *Egyptian Law of Waqf*, to protect the rights of members of the nuclear family, was further reinforced by *Articles 27–29*. *Article 27* asserted the right of a wife to stipulate in her *waqf* that her husband's entitlement will cease should he divorce her or take an additional wife.

Articles 28–29 sought to parallel the *Law of Testamentary Dispositions* in protecting the rights of orphaned grandchildren. The new law permits the founder of *waqf* to grant to the children of his predeceased son or daughter an entitlement in his *waqf* equivalent to the obligatory share rightfully due his deceased child under *Article 24*, if the child had been alive at his father's (the founder's) death.[31]

As a result of all the foregoing regulations, the intention of the *Egyptian Law of Waqf* to protect the rights of a founder's immediate family and to bring the law of *waqf* more into line with reforms in inheritance and testamentary bequest was accomplished. Consequently, *waqf* was prevented from circumventing the reform introduced in succession and testamentary dispositions.

Despite the reforms of 1946, however, only six years later, on September 14, 1952, shortly after the revolution, the Egyptian government abolished all family *waqfs*. *Waqf* property was distributed among the beneficiaries in shares proportionate to their entitlement under the *waqf*.

This radical departure from traditional Muslim law resulted from continued criticism of the *waqf* and the claim that the reform legislation did not significantly eradicate the economic and social injustices caused by its abuse and misapplication in contemporary Egyptian society.

A review of the reforms in inheritance, bequests, and *waqf* reveal two general aims: first to protect the rights of *Quranic* heirs and second, to strengthen the rights of members in the immediate family.

The original purpose of *Quranic* inheritance legislation had been to insure the rights of heirs by establishing fixed shares *(faraid)* to which they were absolutely entitled. Among the principal beneficiaries were wives and daughters of the deceased. Through the centuries, however, certain practices and abuses had arisen which compromised the rights of the *Quranic* heirs. Reform measures, following the *Quranic* intent, sought to assure the protection of heirs. Legislation was passed which permitted testamentary bequests of up to one-third of an estate to heirs as well as non-heirs. Furthermore, to prevent the circumvention of the rights of heirs through improper use of *waqf,* several regulations were introduced: first, all stipulations contrary to the spirit of the *Shariah* were null and void; second, in all *waqfs* exceeding one-third of the estate, *Quranic* heirs were entitled to the equivalent of their "fixed shares;" third, a *waqf* of all the founder's property must go to descendants, parents or spouse before any others. Finally, to protect an heir as well as the heir's descendants against a *waqf* created for the wrong purpose (disinheritance), all *waqfs* were no longer perpetual.

Strengthening the rights of the more immediate family over the more remote agnates in the extended family is the second general purpose of the reforms. Legislation was introduced to insure the inheritance rights of collaterals (brothers and sisters) of the deceased and to prevent their exclusion from inheritance by an uncle. In addition, provision was made for the protection of orphaned grandchildren of the deceased. Following the spirit of the *Quranic* "Verse of Bequest" which encouraged provision for needy relatives, the law of "obligatory bequest" was enacted to guarantee orphaned grandchildren of the deceased a share equivalent to that portion which their deceased father would have inherited had he lived. A similar concern is evident in the law of *waqf* which enabled a grandfather to create a *waqf* for his orphaned grandchild equivalent to the share due the grandchild's deceased parent.

In general, the desire to permit greater provision for members of the immediate family is also seen in the laws which allow testamentary bequests in favor of heirs and encourage *waqfs* in favor of descendants, parents and the spouse (or spouses) of the founder.

LEGAL REFORM IN INDIA-PAKISTAN

Beginnings of Reform

In India-Pakistan, as in Egypt, Muslim reform was due to an internal process within the Muslim community and to the external stimulus of Western presence and criticism.

The year 1857 is a focal point for the history of Islam in India-Pakistan[32] for it marked the *terminus ad quem* of the decline of the Mughal Empire. A veiled truth now became a clear reality. Although there had theoretically been a Mughal sultan, in fact the British had been the predominant economic and political power since the early part of the eighteenth century. In 1857 the last Muslim hope of casting off the yoke of British domination died with the failure of what the British called the "Sepoy Mutiny" or what Hindu and Muslim historians refer to as "the first War of Independence." The resultant condition of the Muslim community after this failure has been fittingly described by I. H. Qureshi as "the lowest depths of broken pride."[33]

Prior to 1857 the Muslims, who had constituted the ruling class, had found it difficult to adjust to the changes introduced by the British—the substitution of the official language from Persian to English and the introduction of a Western educational system. The general reluctance of the Muslim community to avail themselves of new educational facilities meant their relative disassociation from the educational and technological changes occurring in India. For example, between 1835 and 1870 the proportion of Hindus (who had generally accepted British reforms) to Muslims in government service was seven to one.[34] Both their inferior status in society and the failure of their last attempts to free

themselves from the British brought the Muslim community to
what Ahmad Khan described as a "state of utter ruin."[35]

Muslim Reformers

Just as the religio-political concerns of the eighteenth
century in India had produced the reformer Shah Wali Allah
(1703–1763), the political crisis of the nineteenth century produced Sayyid Ahmad Khan. Responding to his people's plight,
Ahmad Khan recognized the need for a revival of the Muslim
community through modernization. Like his Egyptian counterpart, Muhammad Abduh, Khan endeavored to show that there
need not be a conflict between Islam and modern thought, that
reason and religion were entirely compatible. Influenced by the
rationalist tradition in Islam advocated earlier by reform thinkers
such as Wali Allah, as well as by the Enlightenment in Europe,
Khan viewed Islam as the religion of reason and nature. Like
Abduh, he wished to provide the Muslim community with a
rationale for accepting and harnessing the strengths of modern
science and technology: "Today we are, as before, in need of a
modern *ilm al-kalam*, by which we should ... show that they
[modern sciences] are in conformity with the articles of Islamic
faith."[36] To accomplish this his approach was both theoretical and
practical. On the theoretical level, claiming the right of *ijtihad*
(individual interpretation), Khan wrote prolifically, producing his
own commentary on the *Quran*, as well as many writings on legal
reform.[37] Like Tahtawi and Abduh in Egypt, he recognized the
need for educational reform and devoted much time and energy to
its practical implementation. He established a scientific society for
the translation and introduction of works on modern Western
sciences (1864) and most importantly, founded the Anglo-
Muhammadan Oriental College at Aligarh (1874) which was mod-
elled on the British university system at Cambridge. The
Muhammadan Anglo-Oriental Educational Conference was established in 1886. It promoted Western education in Muslim India
and advocated women's education.

Although Ahmad Khan had chiefly concerned himself
with religious and general educational reform, one issue in the

social realm, his position on polygamy, is especially significant. As did Muhammad Abduh, Ahmad Khan utilized *Quranic* verses (IV:2–3, 128) to argue that the marriage ideal in Islam is monogamy since man is incapable of living equally with more than one wife at one time.

However, it was Mumtaz Ali, a scholar of the Deoband Theological School who had become associated with Ahmad Khan, who championed the social aspect of reform in India-Pakistan. Ali's special concern for women's rights led to the publishing of the journal *Tahdhib al-nisa* through which he expressed his views. Mumtaz Ali asserted the need for equality of women with men in marriage and social customs. Like his Egyptian counterpart, Qasim Amin, he stressed the right of equal educational opportunities for women which would then make for better marriages between intellectually equal companions. Ali refuted the anti-feminist exegesis of some classical scholars, maintaining that their interpretations reflected not the meaning of the *Quranic* text, but the customs and mores of the exegetes' own times. In language strikingly similar to Qasim Amin, Mumtaz Ali denounced most of the marriages in Muslim India as loveless servitude endured by women whose inferior position was due to their lack of education and subjection to marriage laws and customs that needed fundamental reform. He criticized child marriages and arranged marriages, asserting that marriage must be based on love and free choice. Ali also followed Khan's position regarding polygamy as a tolerated institution which must in contemporary society give way to the *Quranic* ideal—monogamy.[38]

While Mumtaz Ali provided the modernist social critique for reform, Chiragh Ali, a close protege of Ahmad Khan, spoke more directly to the need for reform of family law to implement needed social changes.

For Chiragh Ali, Islam is distinct from any particular social system. Failure to recognize this had led Muslims in the past to identify their social system and its institutions with the *Quran*, and thus to regard them as ideal.[39]

The law books of the four Sunni schools reflect the social system of Muslim society during the period of their formation. However, since society has changed, Chiragh Ali argued, Muslim law must also be updated to meet new social needs. Thus, the legal manuals of the schools are not immutable sources to be blindly imitated *(taqlid)*. If Muslim family law is viewed in the proper historical context, *Quranic* reforms regarding women's position in marriage, divorce, inheritance vis à vis pre-Islamic practices, will be seen as truly radical: "Islam ... changed the attitude towards women to one of respect, kindness and courtesy. The Muslim law of inheritance, giving a woman exclusive right to her own property, compares favourably with the British law. Man's superiority is recognized by the *Quran* only in matters relating to his natural physical attributes.[40]

These *Quranic* intents and commands (the spirit and letter of its laws) were diverted through the ages by the classical jurists who, in areas such as polygamy and divorce, developed laws which reflected customary practices often at odds with the *Quran*. Ali believed that an overhauling of traditional Islamic law to eliminate anachronistic customary practices alien to the *Quran* was essential to the modernization of the Muslim community[41]

Anglo-Muhammadan Law

The practice of traditional Muslim law in India-Pakistan in the early stages of British rule was unimpaired by foreign intervention. Although many changes came about in other areas, the judicial attitude of the British was characterized by non-interference with the prevailing legal system. Traditional Hanafi law, which had been authoritative under the Mughal dynasty, remained in force. Gradually, however, mere British presence changed to an assertion of British power, especially at the end of the eighteenth century when the British East India Company became more involved in the political and legal life of the country in order to protect its own interests. Initial interference occurred with *Regulation II of 1772*, the reorganization of the court system by which English law was applied in the British Presidency towns. In general, however, Muslims and Hindus continued to be governed by their respective religious laws in all matters.

This situation remained until the latter half of the nineteenth century when the application of Muslim law was narrowed even further by the enactment in 1862 of the *India Penal*

Code and the *Code of Criminal Procedure*. Moreover, portions of the civil code were also codified. As a result of such measures, Islamic law in the Indian subcontinent, as had happened in the Middle East, came to be restricted principally to the domain of family law.

In addition to legislation, the functioning of the courts themselves is of critical importance for legal reform in India-Pakistan. Since judges were either Britains or Muslims trained in British law, English legal principles and concepts were often introduced when, due to language deficiencies, knowledge of traditional (Arabic) legal texts was lacking or when justice and equity seemed to necessitate a departure from traditional law. More importantly, the Indian courts, following the British practice, operated on a case-law system of legally binding precedents. This was a direct departure from Islamic legal practice in which the judge was simply to apply the law. The changes in substantive law resulting from the use of such precedents, as well as the adoption of English juristic methods, led to a legal practice so influenced by the British that it has come to be called "Anglo-Muhammedan Law."

Pre-Partition Muslim Family Law Reform

Paternity and Putative Widowhood

The first important changes in Muslim family law in the Indian subcontinent occurred with the passage of the *Indian Evidence Act of 1872*, which substantially reflected English law in its two areas of reform, establishing paternity and putative widowhood. These reforms, only implemented in Egypt sixty years later, were quite progressive. Regarding paternity, *Section 112* established a presumption of legitimacy for a child born during a valid marriage or within 280 days of its dissolution unless non-access is proved. However, children born after 280 days from the date of the divorce may be declared legitimate by the court on the basis of medical evidence or other substantiated evidence. Following English law, the new law decreed that a child born within days after the marriage is presumed to be the legitimate child and heir of the husband. This rule departed from the six-months maximum norm of the classical legal tradition which was not reformed in Egypt until 1943.[42]

The second change in family law introduced by this act concerned the minimum time necessary for the court to declare putative widowhood. The caution of the Hanafi law, which required a period of ninety years from the husband's date of birth to elapse before declaring a missing husband legally dead, was deemed excessive and unjust. The Act decreed that after a seven-years absence, if attempts to find the husband failed, the court may issue a decree of death and, in effect, declare putative widowhood.

Child Marriage

In the areas of marriage and divorce, additional reforms in family law did not occur until 1929 when the *Child Marriage Restraint Act* sought to limit child marriage, a social ill even more common in the Indian subcontinent than in Egypt.[43] Minimum marital ages of sixteen years for girls and eighteen years for boys were established. The Act provided penalties for any male over twenty-one years who marries a child and for the parent or guardian who promotes, permits, or fails to prevent such a child marriage.[44] Most importantly, the courts were empowered to issue an injunction against a child marriage on the basis of a substantiated complaint *(Section 12.1)*.

Despite the prohibition and penalties, child marriages still remained valid, although they were considered illicit. While an attempt was made to curb a social ill, as in Egypt, lawmakers avoided countering an established regulation. The discouragement of an abuse rather than its outlaw was preferred.

Wife's Right of Divorce

Years passed before additional family law reform was implemented. While Egypt had granted some relief to women through the reform of divorce regulations in 1920 and 1929, such legislation did not occur in the Indian subcontinent until 1939 with *The Dissolution of Muslim Marriages Act.* Ostensibly the Act intended to *"consolidate and clarify the provisions of Muslim Law relating to suits for dissolution of marriage by women . . . and to remove doubts as to the effect of the renunciation of Islam by a married Muslim woman on her marriage tie."*[45] The real purpose of the Act, like that of comparable Egyptian legislation, was to render reforms which would improve the status of women and grant them some judicial relief through establishing additional grounds for divorce, most of which were not recognized by Hanafi law, which was the official law followed by the courts of the subcontinent:

> There is no provision in the Hanafi Code of Muslim Law en-
> abling a married Muslim woman to obtain a decree from the
> Courts dissolving her marriage in case the husband neglects to
> maintain her, makes her life miserable by deserting or persist-
> ently maltreating her or certain other circumstances. The ab-
> sence of such a provision has entailed unspeakable misery to
> innumerable Muslim women in British India. Legislation, then,
> became necessary in order to relieve the sufferings of countless
> Muslim women.[46]

To the two grounds recognized by the Hanafi school, viz. the husband's impotence and the option of puberty, were added a husband's desertion, failure to maintain, failure to perform marital obligations, severe or chronic (physical or mental) defects and cruelty or maltreatment towards his wife. In addition, the 1939 legislation, in a renewed attempt to limit the occurrence of child marriages, broadened one of the traditional grounds for divorce, the option of puberty. Originally the option of puberty in Hanafi law governed all situations in which a minor was given in marriage by someone other than the father or grandfather.[47] Now a female minor given in marriage by her father or grandfather before age fifteen[48] was granted the right to repudiate that marriage any time before reaching eighteen years of age, provided the marriage was not consummated.[49]

    In some of the new grounds for divorce, the Pakistan reforms proved less far-reaching than those of Egypt. For exam-
ple, a wife could only claim desertion as grounds if her husband

was a missing person. However, the reform did lessen the waiting period for a deserted wife's divorce from the traditional ninety years after a husband's birth, to a simple requirement that the whereabouts of the husband have not been known for a four-year period *(Section 2.1). By comparison, the earlier Egyptian reform of 1929 had granted the wife a divorce after one year of her husband's unwarranted absence.* [50] Furthermore, no provision was made for divorce in cases of desertion due to a husband's unwarranted absence and so the importance of the presence of the husband to preserve a marriage was not recognized.

Maintenance was another ground for divorce. *Section 2.11* decreed that non-support for a period of two years is sufficient grounds for a divorce suit. A grace period was provided during which time the husband could satisfy the court that he would perform his conjugal duties and if this occurred, the decree would be set aside *(Section 2.ix.b)*.

Again, while improving the lot of Muslim women in the subcontinent, this law falls short of the coverage provided by *Egyptian Law No. 25, 1920.* Unlike that of Egypt and many other Middle Eastern countries, the law of Pakistan, in fact, penalizes women by requiring them to suffer two years of non-support before they may file for divorce. Furthermore, maintenance is not recognized as a cumulative debt as it is in Egyptian law, and thus a husband who indicates a willingness to pay present maintenance avoids the divorce as well as payment of the past due maintenance.

Another difference is the issue of a husband's imprisonment. Egyptian reform treated imprisonment as a form of desertion and therefore allowed a divorce suit after a one-year absence (the minimum term for all desertion suits) in cases where the husband was serving a minimum sentence of three years. The Pakistan law treats this as an issue of maintenance, stipulating that a woman whose husband has received a final sentence for a minimum of seven years is entitled to an immediate divorce *(Section 2.iii)*. While the minimum sentence requirement (seven years) is longer in Pakistan than in Egypt (three years), the Pakistani wife may obtain her divorce at once without the Egyptian one-year waiting period, thus gaining immediate relief.

Chronic defects (physical and mental) were also recognized as grounds for divorce. A woman is entitled to sue for divorce if her husband has been insane for two years or is suffering from leprosy or a virulent venereal disease.[51]

Finally, a major reform occurred with the inclusion of cruelty *(darar)* as a ground for divorce. Cruelty, as defined in the law, amounted to physical mistreatment or mental anguish. The six subclauses which accompany this regulation provide great breadth. A wife may obtain a divorce if her husband:

1. habitually assaults her or makes her life miserable by cruelty of conduct even if such conduct does not amount to physical ill treatment;
2. associates with women of evil repute or leads an infamous life;
3. attempts to force her to lead an immoral life;
4. disposes of her property or prevents her exercising her legal rights over it;
5. obstructs her in the observance of her religious profession or practice; or
6. has more wives than one and does not treat her with equality in accordance with the injunctions of the Quran *(Section 2.viii)*.

This last subclause is the one instance in which the Indian reform followed Maliki rules more closely than the Egyptian reform legislation which did not include the stipulation regarding equitable treatment.

However, although the reformers claimed to be substituting Maliki principles where Hanafi principles were found wanting, they completely omitted the rather detailed Maliki procedures for using arbitrators which the Egyptian reforms included for all maltreatment cases.[52]

Besides differences in their substantive reforms, Pakistan and Egypt must also be contrasted in the method by which divorce is granted. *The Dissolution of Muslim Marriage Act* adopted judicial decree *(faskh,* recission) rather than Maliki law's judicial repudiation *(talaq)* which was used by the *Egyptian Law No. 25 of 1929.* This difference has practical consequences, since the *talaq* used by Egypt is a revocable repudiation which only becomes final at the end of the *iddah* period. *Faskh,* adopted by Pakistan, becomes final upon its issuance by the Court. It is irrevocable and bypasses the *iddah* period with its provisions for reconciliation and maintenance.

Finally, a clear departure from traditional teaching occurs in the fourth section of Pakistan's law which decreed that a Muslim woman's renunciation of Islam or conversion to a faith other than Islam shall not dissolve her marriage. This particular reform reflects the lot of women prior to this divorce legislation. Lacking sufficient means for relief from intolerable marital situations, some Muslim women were renouncing Islam or nominally claiming conversion to another faith in order to qualify under traditional Hanafi law for a dissolution of their marriage.

Post-Partition Family Law Reforms

Reform Through Judicial Precedent

Despite the reforms rendered by the *Dissolution of Muslim Marriage Act,* inequity still remained, for there were many marital situations in which the wife could not fulfill all the requirements of the specific grounds recognized in the *Act of 1939.* Women entrapped by marriages in which incompatibility of the partners made their union an unjust hardship lacked the right to free themselves through divorce, a right that men had always enjoyed.

Traditional Hanafi law did not recognize incompatibility of temperaments as a legitimate ground for a wife to seek a *khul* divorce. This position was reaffirmed in 1952 by the Pakistan Supreme Court in the case of Sayeeda Khanam v. Muhammad Sami.[53] In a Full Bench decision the court observed: "if the wives were allowed to dissolve their marriage without consent of their husbands by merely giving up their dowers, paid or promised to be paid, the institution of marriage would be meaningless as there would be no stability attached to it."[54]

However, by 1959 this position was changed in Balquis Fatima v. Najm-ul-Ikram Qureshi, by the High Court of Lahore. The Court asserted its right to grant a *khul* divorce where serious incompatibility made a harmonious marriage impossible. According to Hanafi law, a *khul* divorce was extra judicial, based on mutual agreement and, most importantly, dependent upon the husband's consent for its validity.[55] However, basing themselves on the *Quran:* "If ye [judges] do indeed fear that they would be unable to keep the limits ordained by God, there is no blame on either of them if she give something for her freedom" (II:229), the court's interpretation was that the judge has the power to separate the spouses and so dissolve their marriage. Thus the court, through its interpretation of Islamic sources, departed from traditional Hanafi law and allowed judicial dissolution of a marriage by a judge upon evidence that: "the limits of God will not be observed, that is, in their relations to one another, the spouses will not obey God, that a harmonious married state as envisaged by Islam, will not be possible."[56] The requirements set for a wife seeking such a divorce are (1) showing that incompatibility prevented a harmonious marriage, and (2) returning her dower. The Maliki school had allowed a dissolution on similar grounds by arbitrators appointed to examine and resolve a case of serious marital discord either through reconciliation, or where this proved impossible, dissolution of the marriage. However, the Pakistan High Court in no way followed or prescribed the detailed procedural steps prescribed by the Malikis.

That the court sought to remedy the social injustice suffered by women can be seen in the Justices' observation that "The marriage has to be terminated because it is not a reasonably possible view that a marriage must continue even though the husband misbehaves, or is unable to perform his obligation or for no fault of the wife it would be cruel to continue it."[57] This position of the High Court was given the highest approbation in 1967 when, in the case of Khurshid Bibi v. Mohamed Amin, the Supreme Court, the highest judicial authority in Pakistan, declared that Khurshid Bibi was entitled to a divorce upon returning her dower to her husband. Thus, while the right of the man to repudiate his wife has remained unfettered, the granting of a unilateral *khul* divorce to a woman in case of incompatibility represents significant headway in achieving a balance of rights.

Reforms in Muslim family law that occurred in the Indian Subcontinent prior to 1947 continued in effect in both India and the new Muslim nation of Pakistan after the Partition; legal reform in the new state also continued.

Reform Through Legislation

On August 4, 1955, eight years after Pakistan's founding, the Commission on Marriage and Family Laws was established to review Muslim family law to determine whether changes were necessary.

The commission was composed of three men, three women and one religious scholar (to represent the *ulama*). Their work resulted in the *Report of the Commission on Marriage and Family Laws of June, 1956*. The Report represented the recommendations of the six laymen majority. However, shortly thereafter in August 1956, Maulana Ihtisham-al-Haq, a religious scholar (alim, pl. ulama) and a traditionalist, published a vigorous dissenting report taking issue with virtually every major recommendation of his colleagues on the commission. There then ensued an extended debate between modernists and traditionalists.

In March of 1961 many of the recommendations of the Commission on Marriage and Family Laws were embodied in *The Muslim Family Laws Ordinance VIII of 1961*, which introduced reforms in marriage, polygamy, divorce, maintenance, and succession. However, the effect of conservative opposition to reforms can also be seen in certain provisions or qualifications that weakened the effect of the reforms and the omission of such areas as *waqf* (religious endowments) reform.

Marriage Registration

To avoid the difficulties of false claims resulting from oral contracts, Pakistan, like Egypt before it, introduced the requirement of written registration of marriages and created the office of *Nikah* (Marriage) Registrar to grant marriage licenses and oversee the registration of marriages *(Section 5.1–2)*. Failure to report marriages to the Registrar became punishable by fine and/or imprisonment.

However, these restrictions were considerably weakened by the fact that failure to register a marriage did not affect the validity of the marriage and the maximum sentence for neglecting such registration was only three months. The effectiveness of this law was further hampered since, in contrast to the *Egyptian Law of 1931,*[58] judicial relief was not denied to unregistered marriages in Pakistan. Thus, suits involving marriage, divorce, paternity and inheritance in unregistered marriages were admissable in court.

Polygamy

Reform legislation was also introduced to limit polygamy. The law required the creation of an Arbitration Council, a new institution to handle polygamous marriage, divorce and maintenance. A married man who wishes to contract another marriage is now required to obtain written permission from the Council. Each applicant is required to state the reasons for the proposed marriage and the attitudes of his wife or wives toward giving their consent to the marriage (*Section 6.2*). The Chairman then organizes the Arbitration Council by asking the parties involved to nominate their representatives. Upon examination of the application, and if convinced that the proposed marriage is "necessary and just," permission is granted (*Section 6.3*). In determining what is necessary and just, the *West Pakistan Rules Under the Muslim Family Laws Ordinance, 1961* suggests that the Council consider "Sterility, physical infirmity, physical unfitness for conjugal relations, willful avoidance of a decree for restitution of conjugal rights, or insanity on the part of the existing wife" (*Section 14*). Decisions of the Council are subject to appeal (*Section 6.4*).

A husband who fails to comply with the above regulations is penalized in the following ways: he must immediately repay the entire dower to his existing wife or wives; his wives have the right to immediate dissolution of their marriage;[59] he can be imprisoned for up to one year and/or fined up to 5,000 rupees (*Section 6.5.a−b*). Furthermore, marriages contracted without the Council's permission are denied official registration and thus all cases which might arise from such a marriage are denied judicial relief (*Section 6.1*). However, despite these sanctions, all such marriages are still valid.

Divorce

As previously noted, the *Dissolution of Muslim Marriages Act of 1939*, although supposedly following Maliki law, had in several important instances ignored Maliki doctrine concerning the grounds for divorce. Unlike similar Egyptian legislation, the Pakistan law has failed to include the detailed procedures for arbitration in cases where the wife sues for divorce on the basis of cruelty or maltreatment. This is especially noteworthy since the Maliki doctrine is based on a *Quranic* injunction (IV:35).[60]

The *Ordinance of 1961* remedied this deficiency by employing the Arbitration Council for all cases of divorce *(Section 8)*. To discourage hasty exercise of the husband's right of repudiation *(talaq)*, this reform legislation required written notice to the Chairman as well as to the wife *(Section 7.1)*. A ninety day waiting period is required during which the Council will seek to reconcile the couple *(Section 7.4)*. The divorce does not take effect until the ninety day period has elapsed or, if the wife is pregnant, until the completion of pregnancy *(Section 7.3 and 5)*.

Although failure to observe the above procedures is punishable by fine and/or imprisonment, the penalties are relatively light (up to one year or a fine of up to 5,000 rupees) *(Section 7.2)*. This, coupled with the fact that failure to comply with the regulations regarding the Arbitration Council has no effect on the validity of the divorce, has diminished its effectiveness.

Paralleling an earlier Egyptian reform, Pakistan's reform legislation also decreed that all divorces are revocable and thus remarriage without an intervening marriage is possible, (unless this is the third such divorce). This reform returned to the *Quranic* law requiring three divorces, separated by a waiting period, for an irrevocable divorce. As a result, it eliminated the abuse of *talaq al-bidah* which had caused much social injustice by circumventing the *Quranic* waiting period *(iddah)*. It also eliminated the need for both parties who had been divorced by *talaq al-bidah* to arrange for an intervening marriage before their remarriage was possible *(Section 7.6)*.

In the *Ordinance of 1961* the Arbitration Council was employed in yet another area—a wife's claim of maintenance. The procedure involving the Council is similar to that used for polygamy and divorce cases. Prior to the passage of this law, several remedies were available to a wife who attempted to recover maintenance due her: application under 488 of the *Criminal Procedure Code*, a suit for recovery of maintenance, or, if two years had passed without maintenance, a suit for dissolution of the marriage. Now the Council had broad powers to review claims involving non-support or inadequate support and to award or refuse maintenance.

The All-Pakistan Women's Association continued to agitate for further reforms in marriage and divorce. The following were proposed as amendments to the *Family Laws Ordinance of 1961:*

1. That in accordance with the *Quranic* sayings notice of the intention of divorce should be communicated to the Authorities before the actual divorce notice, so that there is a better chance of avoiding divorce. Also the wife should stay in her husband's home during her *iddat* so that by remaining together there may be some chance of their reconciliation.

2. The *Family Laws Ordinance* is silent on custody. The law should provide that whilst deciding about the custody of the children of broken homes, the court should keep in view not only the welfare of the children but also the wishes of such children.

3. That women who are divorced by their husbands without any reasonable cause or without their being at fault should be allowed reasonable maintenance by the husband as enjoyed [*sic.*] by the *Holy Quran*. "For divorced women maintenance should be provided on a reasonable scale. This is a duty on the righteous" (II:24).

4. Separate courts should be established (in which only family dispute cases should be tried) for family and marital disputes in all districts and cases be heard and decided by a special judge within a prescribed period of three months.[61]

Only the fourth proposal was acted upon. *The West Pakistan Family Courts Act, 1964*, established separate Family Courts "for the expeditious settlement and disposal of disputes relating to marriage and family affairs and for matters connected therewith."[62]

Dower and Dowry

The only other significant family law reforms in Pakistan since 1964 have concerned dower *(mahr)* and dowry *(jihaz)*. While dower is a payment due a wife from her husband at marriage, dowry is the obligation of the bride's family. In 1965, a High Court decision ruled that since willful non-payment of maintenance is grounds for divorce, so too willful non-payment of dower is grounds for divorce.[63]

Dowry, although not rooted in Islamic law, is a firmly established custom. It consists of property such as clothing, money, and jewelry, which the bride's family is obligated to provide. Although the dowry theoretically belongs to the bride, it usually passes to the husband and his family upon marriage and, so, is often an important factor in arranging marriages. In the Indian subcontinent, dowry and lavish weddings have long been recognized as creating serious social problems, since family pride and a desire to provide a suitable marriage often result in the bride's family incurring substantial debts.[64] In 1967, the *West Pakistan Dowry (Prohibition On Display) Act* was enacted to alleviate this problem. The law affirms a woman's right as "absolute owner" to her dowry and bridal gifts, i.e, property given to the bride by the bridegroom or his parents *(Section 4.1)*. It also forbids the display of dowry and bridal gifts. However, the law did not address the more serious problems of excessive dowry demands by perspective husbands, and lavish weddings. It was these concerns that led to passage of the *Dowry and Bridal Gifts (Restriction) Act* in 1976 which sought to regulate (1) dowry and bridal gifts; (2) presents, i.e, any property (other than dowry or bridal gifts) given to either spouse; and (3) wedding feasts. Its major stipulations included affirming the bride as sole owner of the dowry, bridal gifts and presents; limiting the total value of dowry and bridal gifts as well as presents to 5,000 rupees or $500 *(Section 3.1)*; restricting the amount of money expended on wedding feasts to 2,500 rupees or $250 *(Section 6)*; requiring that all dowry, bridal gifts and presents be displayed *(Section 7)* and that the bride and groom's parents submit lists of wedding expenses, dowry, bridal gifts, and presents to the Registrar of Marriage *(Sections 7 and 8)*.

Succession

From the juristic viewpoint, the most noteworthy reform in the *Muslim Family Law Ordinance of 1961* concerned the law of succession. *Section 4* modified the traditional law of inheritance by introducing the principle of full representation for orphaned grandchildren of the deceased *(praepositus)*, i.e., they are to receive "a share equivalent to the share which such son or daughter as the case may be, would have received, if alive" *(Section 4)*.

Although the Pakistan reform accomplished the same end as the Egyptian reform, their methods differed. Egyptian reformers, always more juristically conscious, avoided direct intervention in the law of succession; they chose instead to insure the rights of orphaned grandchildren through the introduction of the principle of "obligatory bequests" in the law of testamentary dispositions. Such a change had some juristic basis among traditional authorities. However, Pakistan's reformers, responding to the same social need, chose to meet this problem by legislating a reform in the law of succession despite the lack of traditional authority.

Religious Endowment (Waqf)

The history of *waqf* in India-Pakistan proves interesting both from the viewpoint of jurisprudence and the reform of substantive law.

As was mentioned earlier, the law of the subcontinent constitutes its own unique species — Anglo-Muhammedan Law. The normal procedure of the court in family law cases called for reference to authoritative texts of the Hanafi school in rendering decisions. However, under British influence, the judges in practice also utilized the legal principle of equity. In cases where the bench decided that application of the letter of the law compromised equity, the judges might not follow it. The exercise of this judicial independence led to a major legal crisis at the end of the nineteenth century in the case of Abul Fata Mahomed Ishak v. Russomoy Dhur Chowdhry. The case concerned two brothers who created a family *waqf* whose income was to pass on to their children and then to their descendants until the family was extinct.

Then, the usufruct of the *waqf* was to be used for charitable purposes.

While the lower court initially confirmed the validity of this family *waqf,* the High Court in 1894 reversed the decision. On further appeal, the British Privy Council upheld the reversal of the High Court.

The decision of the Judicial Committee of the Privy Council was based on the belief that such family *waqfs* provided no substantial gift to the poor. In fact, such a gift was illusory due to its remoteness:

> It is . . . illusory to make a provision for the poor under which they are not entitled to receive a rupee till after the total extinction of a family; possibly not for hundreds of years . . . certainly not as long as there exists on the earth one of those objects whom the donor really cared to maintain in a high position. Their Lordships agree that the poor have been put into this settlement merely to give it a colour of piety, and so to legalize arrangements meant to serve for the aggrandizement of a family.[65]

In effect, then, the court had criticized the traditional law of *waqf* and rejected it in rendering a decision. Following the British legal principle of justice and equity, the justices had not simply interpreted and applied the authoritative texts (as is required under Islamic law) but rather had arrived at a new conclusion. Thus, the new criteria for judging the validity of a *waqf* would be a determination that the gift to charity was substantial and not merely nominal.

As might be expected, a storm of protest led by such notables as Ameer Ali, the famous legal scholar and judge, rose from the Muslim community. Ali's work on Islamic law had often been cited by the courts in their decisions. However, in this case the justices had rejected his defense of the *waqf* system. Despite protests, the decision of the Judicial Committee remained a binding legal precedent until 1913 and the passage of the *Waqf Act of 1913* or *Mussalman Waqf Validating Act, 1913.* This act, in effect, reversed the position of the High Court and the Judicial Committee and restored the Islamic law of family *waqf.* Addressing itself directly to the doubts regarding the validity of family *waqf* raised by judicial decisions, the law stated that "No such *waqf* [i.e. family *waqf*] shall be deemed to be invalid merely because the benefit reserved therein for the poor or other religious, pious or charitable purpose of a permanent nature is postponed until after the extinction of the family, children or descendants of the person creating the *waqf.*"[66] Thus, through legislative intervention, the Muslim law of family *waqf* was restored. But the saga of *waqf* legislation continues even further. In 1922, in the case of Khajeh Solehman v. Salimullah Bahadur, the Privy Council ruled that the Act of 1913 had not been retroactive and therefore was inoperative regarding all *waqfs* created prior to March, 1913. Again, in order to override judicial legal interpretation, legislative recourse was taken in the passage of the *Waqf Validating Act, XXXII of 1930* which declared that the *Waqf Act of 1913* was retroactive to *waqfs* created prior to March 7, 1913.

Since Partition, the only major legislation in Pakistan affecting *waqf* has been the *West Pakistan Land Reform Regulation of 1959*. Within this land reform legislation was a provision that declared all lands not specifically dedicated for religious or charitable purposes shall cease to form part of a *waqf* (Para. 10.1–2). Otherwise, the law of *waqf* remains substantially unchanged. There has been no reform of the *waqf* system comparable to that of Egypt. The result is a system which continues to favor the extended family over the nuclear family. The *waqf* system in Pakistan, then, can still be used by the founder to circumvent the Muslim law of succession and exclude heirs, principally women. Furthermore, inequities resulting from such discrimination against female heirs will continue to affect the descendants generation after generation since a *waqf* is perpetual.

Summary

Laws were enacted in India-Pakistan to correct abuses in Muslim society by restricting child marriage and granting women the additional Maliki grounds for divorce (failure to pay maintenance, desertion, and cruelty). However, the most significant piece of reform legislation in post-partition Pakistan was the enactment of the *Muslim Family Laws Ordinance of 1961*. Besides abolishing the practice of *talaq al-bidah* and requiring the registration of marriages, reformers tackled three major areas of reform: the restriction of polygamy, the discouragement of hasty divorces, and the settlement of maintenance claims. This was accomplished by officially instituting a procedure recommended by the *Quran* for marital disputes (IV:35). Arbitration Councils were established and, following the spirit of the *Quran*, representatives of the involved parties (husband and wife) were to be its members.

In addition, a direct change was effected in the law of inheritance to insure the rights of orphaned grandchildren to their deceased father's share in his father's estate.

Finally, in a unique action in modern legal reform, the Muslim community, through its legislators, repealed the action of the Privy Council in abolishing *waqf* and reinstituted a long-established Muslim institution.

LEGAL REFORMS: AN OVERVIEW

Contemporary Muslim family law reform in Egypt and Pakistan reflects and reinforces the shift in emphasis from the extended to the nuclear family which has been slowly taking place in modern Muslim society. This is reflected in legislation to improve the status of women and the rights of lineal descendants.

Legislation has been passed in both countries to restrict child marriages and polygamy and, most importantly, to increase the grounds upon which a woman has the right to sue for divorce. Although Egypt had led the Muslim world in women's emancipation and legal reform, little occurred after the 1940's until 1979. Pakistan's *Muslim Family Law Ordinance of 1961* surpassed Egypt in attempting to restrict polygamy and divorce.

The second major purpose of legal reform has been the strengthening of the rights of parents and lineal descendants. Thus, both Egypt and Pakistan have passed legislation providing for the inheritance rights of orphaned grandchildren to their pre-deceased parent's share of the grandparent's estate. However, in three important areas, Pakistan has lagged behind Egypt. Whereas Egyptian reform legislation has made a bequest to an heir or up to one-third of an estate possible, such legislation, which can be beneficial to members of the immediate family and especially wives and daughters, has not been passed in Pakistan. Second, in the law of succession, where brothers and sisters of the deceased could be totally excluded from any inheritance by an uncle, their rights have been insured in Egyptian law. Pakistan has no such legislation. Finally, Egypt initiated extensive reforms of *waqf,* especially in the area of "obligatory entitlements," to prevent an abuse of *waqf* (the bypassing of *Quranic* laws of inheritance). This secured the rights of members of the immediate family, especially daughters. While the *Marriage and Family Laws Commission Report of 1956* had recommended *waqf* reform, the *Muslim Family Laws Ordinance of 1961* omitted it. No further action has taken place since that time.

Beyond Egypt and Pakistan, reforms in other Muslim countries provide some perspective on the extent and possibilities for future reforms. During the intervening decades, other Middle Eastern and North African Muslim countries following Egypt's example not only by emulating her reforms, but also by addressing the issue of polygamy and its restriction. Syria was the first Muslim state to legislate such a restriction. The *Syrian Law of Personal Status of 1953* which had followed Egypt in its family law reforms also included an additional stipulation which requires a Muslim who already has a wife to obtain permission from the court before contracting another marriage. Permission to take an additional wife is contingent upon the court being convinced that the husband is financially capable of assuming this new obligation. Court permission for a polygamous marriage has been adopted by other Muslim countries such as Morocco, Iran, and Iraq.

Tunisia, under President Bourguiba, enacted the most radical legislation in 1957 when polygamy was outlawed entirely. The government argued that (1) polygamy, like slavery, was an institution whose past purpose was no longer acceptable to most people; and (2) the ideal of the *Quran* was monogamy. Here, the position of the Egyptian reformer Muhammad Abduh was espoused, namely, that the *Quranic* permission to take up to four wives (IV:3) was seriously qualified by verse 129: "Ye are never able to be fair and just between women even if that were your ardent desire" (IV:129). Thus, while polygamy was permitted, the

Quranic ideal is monogamy. Furthermore, in modern times, the *Quranic* requirement of equal treatment of wives was deemed impossible.

However, no other Muslim country has followed the Tunisian example. Rather, more limited approaches like those of Syria and Pakistan have predominated. For example, Jordan in 1951, Morocco in 1958 enacted family laws legislation which permits a wife at the time of marriage to include a stipulation in her marital contract which gives her the right to divorce her husband should he subsequently take an additional wife. Justification for such a measure was found in the Hanbali school of law which, unlike the Hanafi school, recognized the placing of such contingent stipulations in a marriage contract. Furthermore, under the Moroccan law, even if such a stipulation is omitted at the time of marriage, a woman can still sue for divorce on the grounds that her husband's second marriage was injurious. This provision was based upon the acceptance of the general principle derived from Quranic interpretation that polygamy is not permitted where any injustice between wives may exist. Similarly, under Iraqi (1959) and Egyptian (1979) reforms, the taking of an additional wife is grounds for the existing wife (wives) to obtain a divorce.

Iran's *Family Protection Act of 1967* provided another approach to protecting the rights of a wife in a polygamous marriage. In addition to requiring that a husband obtain judicial permission based upon proof of financial competence and equal treatment, *Article 2* required that all marriage contracts include an irrevocable power of attorney enabling a wife to divorce her husband if he should take another wife without her consent. What is optional in other Muslim countries was mandated in Iran.

Perhaps the most contested area of reform has been the attempt to transfer the right of divorce from the Muslim husband to the courts. Whereas traditional Islamic law recognized a Muslim male's unilateral right of divorce, modern family law legislation has subordinated his exercise of this right to the jurisdiction of the courts. In countries like Syria (1953), Morocco (1958) and Iraq (1979), court permission is required before a husband may repudiate his wife. In Iran (1967), a husband may not divorce his wife until he has obtained a "Certificate of Irreconcilability" from the court. Pakistan (1961), as has been seen, has a more modified law which simply stipulates that the Union (Arbitration) Council must be informed (of a repudiation) by the husband, and that a divorce does not become effective until ninety days after it has been reported to the Council and attempts at reconciliation have failed. However, in all the above cases, failure to comply with the law does not render the divorce invalid but simply illicit. The only exception to this process is Tunisia (1956) which declared an extra-judicial divorce invalid. Therefore, in most Muslim countries a husband who is willing to face possible imprisonment, a court fine, or pay his ex-wife compensation, may choose to ignore the reform laws and exercise his traditional unfettered right of divorce. Reform legislation, therefore, has not invalidated the traditional law but simply sought to restrict it in certain areas.

LEGAL METHODOLOGIES OF REFORM: A CRITICAL ANALYSIS

Egypt

A study of modern Muslim law reform in Egypt reveals three specific legal mechanisms employed to provide an Islamic basis of change: *siyasah shariyyah (shariah rule), takhayyur* (selection), and *talfiq* (patching together).

Since Egyptian reform in family law was accomplished through government legislation, the *siyasah shariyyah* power of the ruler or government was used to provide Islamic or religious justification. This doctrine of Islamic public law grants the political authority the prerogative power, whenever he sees fit, to take administrative steps in the public interest in order to insure a society ruled according to the *Shariah*. Thus, full judicial power rested in the sovereign's hands so that he could determine the organs of legal administration as well as the extent of their jurisdiction. Such discretionary powers were granted the ruler in order to insure that the spirit of *Shariah* rule be present in the state in areas that were either not covered at all or not covered sufficiently by the letter of the law. For example, child marriages could be discouraged by indirect means, namely, restricting the competency of the court to hear only cases in which the spouses were old enough to have received an official marriage certificate.

A more widespread application of *siyasah shariyyah* involved the government's selection of one legal doctrine from among the variant opinions of the four Sunni law schools and its prescribing that it also be applied by the courts. The practice of *takhayyur* (selection, preference) was the basis for this activity. Originally, *takhayyur* referred to the right of a Muslim to select and follow the teaching of a school of law other than his own with regard to a particular transaction. The reformers took the principle and applied it to legislative reform. A major example of this was the Egyptian reform legislation of 1920 and 1929 which established grounds for divorce based on Maliki opinion (See pp. 117–124). The *siyasah* power of the political authority was then invoked to pass legislation which required the courts to apply the "preferred" or "selected" Maliki opinions.

Whereas traditionally *takhayyur* was restricted to selection of the dominant opinion of another law school, the reformers extended it to the adoption of an individual jurist's opinion. This understanding of *takhayyur*, however, did constitute a clear departure from traditional usage which limited "selection" to the dominant opinion of one of the four schools. For example, regarding Egypt's *Law No. 25 of 1929*, jurists wishing to correct an abuse which resulted from the formalistic positions of the predominant views of the four schools, turned to Ibn Taymiyah of the Hanbali school as the main source of the regulation that the effectiveness of conditional expressions of divorce was contingent upon intention and not mere utterance of a divorce formula (See p. 127).

An even more innovative method of reform, from the viewpoint of classical law, was a variation of *takhayyur: talfiq* (patching together). By this eclectic process, the views of various schools or jurists are combined to form a single rule or law. A clear case of *talfiq* may be seen in *Article 17* of Egypt's *Law of Waqf of 1946*.

Egyptian reformers have always scrupulously sought to provide a rationale which formally, at least, appeared to follow *(taqlid)* authoritative teachings of the past. However, the use of *talfiq* in drafting *Article 17* demonstrates the tenuousness of this method. This usage is problematic for two reasons: first, traditionally a condition for the practice of *takhayyur* was that the individual not combine teachings, but rather follow the predominant opinion of another school; and second, the position of schools in this case is applied out of context. The doubtfulness of the reformers' claims is evident since the Hanbali school considered temporary *waqfs* invalid, and so regarded the ownership of beneficiaries to be simply a nominal title. Despite this fact, because they were so anxious to clothe their reform in the mantle of traditional authority, the reformers employed a methodology which claimed formal adherence to past authorities, but actually introduced a substantial material change in the law.

This review of the methodology upon which twentieth century reforms in Egyptian family law have been based shows a deep concern that the legal changes not be viewed as the product of *ijtihad* (reinterpretation). Theoretically, reformers following Muhammad Abduh might advocate Islamic reform through the use of *ijtihad*. In practice, however, Egyptian reforms have been limited to legal mechanisms such as *siyasah shariyyah, takhayyur* and *talfiq* and, as we have seen, these have often been misapplied in order to appear to be following past legal doctrines. While the motive might be laudable, the methodology is questionable. One might argue that given the exigencies of their times, such tactics were justified in order to achieve the required reforms. But the long-range value of such methods is negligible since they do not contribute to a systematic Islamic rationale for legal reform which in the long run would give consistency to substantive legal change. As will be discussed in the next chapter, an Islamic rationale for legal reform can be found in the sources of jurisprudence which were originally responsible for the development of Islamic law.

Pakistan

While the purpose of Muslim reformers in the Indian subcontinent was similar to that of the Egyptians, there were important differences in their methodology which has included both legislative and judicial means.

Legislative change in Pakistan, like that of Egypt, might rest on the *siyasah* power of the government. However, the reformers' use of *takhayyur* was quite different from Egyptian usage, as can be seen in the *Dissolution of Muslim Marriage Act of 1939*. *Takhayyur* was employed with far less consistency than similar Egyptian legislation of 1920 and 1929. Whereas Egyptian laws generally adhered to Maliki doctrine concerning grounds for divorce, the India-Pakistan legislation of 1939 differed from Maliki opinion regarding the scope of desertion, the length of maintenance period (See pp. 162–163), cumulative nature of maintenance (See p. 164), and the lack of detailed procedures regarding arbitration in maltreatment cases (See pp. 165–66). Furthermore, from a traditional juristic point of view, Pakistan's law of 1939 arbitrarily veered from Maliki opinion and Egyptian legislation by prescribing divorce by judicial decree *(faskh)* rather than judicial repudiation *(talaq)*. This variance is significant not only because of its departure from traditional ways, but also because of change in the effective date of a divorce (See pp. 165–66). A divorce by *faskh* results in an immediate final dissolution whereas *talaq* does not take effect until the expiration of the wife's *iddah* (waiting period). Consequently, in a suit involving maintenance under the Egyptian legislation, a reconciliation is possible if during the *iddah* period the husband demonstrates his capability and desire to maintain his wife, whereas Pakistan's law precludes such a reconciliation.

Recent legislative action in Pakistan has demonstrated a new attitude toward change based on social need. Thus the inclusion in the *Muslim Family Laws Ordinance of 1961* of the rule that orphaned grandchildren are entitled to their father's share of a deceased grandfather's estate provides a clear example of reform based upon social need. Whereas the Egyptian jurists in 1946 had achieved reform indirectly by introducing this reform in the law of bequests (within which they would provide a *Quranic* justification), the Pakistan legislators directly reformed the law of inheritance despite a lack of any basis in traditional law. This action was rationalized on the grounds of social desirability and a lack of any prohibition in the primary sources of Islamic law *(Quran* and *Sunnah)*. [67]

A second means of reform peculiar to Anglo-Muhammadan law occurred through the operation of the courts. Technically, the courts of Pakistan were merely to apply the law of authoritative legal manuals, not to create or expand it. [68] However, several factors influenced a departure from classical law. The judiciary was not as learned in legal texts as *qadis* of the Middle East for whom Arabic, the language of legal manuals, was a mother tongue. Most importantly, the justices were, from 1772 on, British. It was only in the late nineteenth and twentieth centuries that any Muslims were appointed to the Bench. In any event, all justices were trained in the British legal system and so British legal principles, especially those of justice and equity were employed. Thus, while traditional law was respected, where it was judged insufficient to issue a "just" decision, the courts supplemented the law (departed from strict adherence to Islamic law). Two primary instances of such judicial legal supplementation concern the inclusion of stipulations in marriage contracts and the rejection of family *waqf*.

With the exception of the Hanbali school, the Sunni schools of law do not admit the inclusion of stipulations or conditions concerning the rights of the marital partners. However, the courts in Indian subcontinent, although committed to follow Hanafi law, have quietly allowed such agreements in Muslim marriage contracts, and this action was not the result of adoption of Hanbali opinion.[69]

The second example of judicial interference with traditional law concerned the law of religious endowment *(waqf)*. In 1894 the Privy Council upheld a high court decision which was contrary to Hanafi law of family *waqf*. However, the court's clear departure from traditional law in rejecting the validity of family *waqf* was later reversed by *waqf* legislation.

The courts of Pakistan have, within the last decade, taken an even bolder position regarding their powers. As mentioned above, although the principles of justice and equity had influenced court decisions, the function and duty of the court had always been recognized in theory as the application of Hanafi law found in classical legal manuals. However, a clear departure from this position occurred in 1964 in a decision rendered by the High Court of Lahore in Khurshid Jan v. Fazal Dad. The question posed by the court was "Can courts differ from the views of *imams* and other jurisconsuls of Muslim law (i.e, the authoritative legal texts) on grounds of public policy, justice, equity, and good conscience."

After an exhaustive study, the court responded that "if

there is no clear rule of decision in *Quranic* and traditional texts...
a court may resort to private reasoning and, in that, will undoubt-
edly be guided by the rules of justice, equity, and good conscience
... views of the earlier jurists and *imams* are entitled to the utmost
respect and cannot be lightly disturbed; but the right to differ from
them must not be denied to the present-day courts."[70] The court's
power to exercise *ijtihad* was again underscored in Zohra Begum
v. Latif Ahmed in which the court departed from rules governing
custody of a minor. The High Court of Lahore reversed the decision of a lower court and instead allowed a mother continued
custody of her children beyond the ages at which they would
usually be turned over to their father. This decision was justified in
terms of the best interests of the child.[71]

The result of these landmark decisions is that the courts of
Pakistan no longer view themselves as restricted to following
(taqlid) the authoritative opinions of the past. Instead, where
justice and equity demand, they may exercise *ijtihad* (resort to
individual reasoning or interpretation) based on the following
criteria: (1) that the decision meets a social need, and (2) that the
regulation is not prohibited by the *Quran* and *Sunnah*.

However, the *ijtihad* of the courts differs from the *ijtihad*
of the past as well as that of many modernists who would base their
ijtihad not only on social need, but also on *Quranic* values. Such
an approach insures the Islamic basis and character of reforms and
distinguishes itself from that of the Pakistani Courts whose
methodological basis seems indistinguishable from that of rational
humanism.

While the reforms introduced through legislation and
judicial decision in Pakistan might have been needed, their lack of
a systematic Islamic rationale creates serious problems. First, it
raises questions as to the Islamic character of the laws and the
relationship of the reforms to the body of traditional law. Second,
following from this unresolved theoretical and methodological
question, the apparent discontinuity of many reforms with traditional *fiqh* brings then under heavy fire from the masses of the
population who tend to be more conservative in outlook. For
example, besides the strong opposition to the recommendations of
the Commission on Marriage and Family Law of 1955 which
delayed legislation until 1961, passage of the *Family Laws Ordi-*

nance was followed by continued discontent and debate. Consequently, in July 1963, the West Pakistan Provincial Assembly passed a resolution recommending the repeal of the Ordinance. With support from A.P.W.A. and other women's organizations, much of the press, the President of Pakistan, and his Law Minister, the bill to repeal the law was defeated in the National Assembly (November 26, 1963) after 20 hours of debate.

The continued vulnerability of those aspects of family law reform which lack a rationale rooted in Islamic jurisprudence is once more evident in Pakistan today. During the latter half of the 1970's, Pakistan, like many other Muslim countries, has experienced a strong re-emergence of Islam in its politics.[72] Islam was used by opposition forces to build a coalition against the government of Zulfikar Ali Bhutto. General Zia ul-Haq, who seized power from Bhutto in a 1977 *coup d'etat*, has continued to appeal to Islam to legitimate his rule. Zia speaks of an Islamic system *(Nizam-i-Islam)* of government which has included the introduction of Islamic measures concerned with taxation *(zakat* and *ushr)*, banking interest *(riba)*, and Quranic punishments *(hudud)*. The Islamic Ideology Council, which consists of government appointed religious and lay experts, serves as an advisory body to the government on Islamic affairs. Among the items on its agenda is revision of several provisions in the *Muslim Family Laws Ordinance of 1961* which are seen as lacking an Islamic rationale. Three provisions in particular have been under consideration: (1) procedures governing notice of divorce and mandated period for reconciliation; (2) the requirement that a husband indicate whether his existing wife has consented to a proposed second marriage; and (3) the stipulation that orphaned grandchildren be awarded that share of their grandparent's estate which would have gone to their predeceased parent.

In conclusion, a review of the methodology of the family law reforms in Egypt and Pakistan shows an *ad hoc*, fragmented approach which has employed questionable *talfiq* (patching together), an incomplete following of *takhayyur* (selection), and a claim to *ijtihad* (reinterpretation) not positively rooted in Islamic values but negatively based on a lack of conflict with any *Quranic* injunction. The lack of consistency in methodology is reflected in the law itself. For example, while an *ad hoc* measure such as the provision for orphaned grandchildren's inheritance rights met a particular need, it disrupted the law of succession in Pakistan. Here, an orphaned granddaughter of the deceased now excludes the collaterals (brothers and sisters) of the deceased from inheritance. However, the deceased's own daughter would not exclude these same collaterals.

The reformers of both countries face the same basic problems. If reform is to be truly accepted by the majority of Muslims in each country, and if they are to produce a law that is both comprehensive and consistently developed, these reforms must be based on a systematic methodology whose Islamic roots can be demonstrated. As will be seen in Chapter 4, the dynamic sources for family law reform already exist in traditional Islamic jurisprudence.

4

A LEGAL METHODOLOGY FOR REFORM

HE TWENTIETH CENTURY HAS BEEN A REMARKABLY SIG-
NIFICANT ERA in the history of Muslim family law in the
areas of both substantive legal reform and jurisprudence proper.
Reinterpretation and reform have occurred in both areas. In the
name of social progress, reform legislation has been enacted to
more equitably meet the changing social and economic needs of
women and the family in modern Muslim society. However, salu-
tary as substantive legal change may be, and noble as reformers'
motives may have seemed, their solutions have been of an *ad hoc*
and piecemeal nature and their legal methodology has been
deficient.[1]

The true effectiveness of existing reforms is dependent
upon their acceptance not simply by those who legislate but by the
entire Muslim community. Thus reforms must be rooted in a
consistent Islamic rationale, one which would demonstrate a link
of continuity between change and past tradition. Jurisprudence,
the legal principles and methods underlying the reforms, must
play a key role since it alone can insure both inner consistency and
historical continuity with the Islamic tradition.

TRADITION AND CHANGE

While tradition plays an important role in most cultures, in Islam it has been elevated to an almost sacrosanct status. The reasons for the eventual "sacralization" of tradition are not difficult to identify. The progressive idealization of the history of Islamic law tended to separate the ideal from the real, the immutable from the mutable. The customary practice *(sunnah)* of Arabia, which was incorporated into Islamic law, came to be equated with the *Sunnah* (practice) of the Prophet and thus it was given an unwarranted, elevated religious status. The acceptance of al-Shafii's formulation of the sources of Islamic law also meant a down-playing of the role of reason in the development of law. In classical jurisprudence, the restriction of reasoning *(ijtihad)* to analogy *(qiyas)* created a sense that law was simply the product of specific *Quranic* and *Sunnah* teachings plus those doctrines clearly derived from the *Quran* and *Sunnah* through the application of *qiyas*. Thus, much of substantive law *(fiqh)*, which was actually based upon human understanding and interpretation, was given a more sacrosanct character. *Ijma* (consensus) also contributed to the process of absolutizing tradition. Although *ijma* served as a check on individual interpretation *(ijtihad)*, the ongoing dynamic, dialectical *ijtihad-ijma* relationship tended to be forgotten. This is reflected in the saying attributed to the Prophet: "My community will never agree on an error." A mechanism created to arrive at authoritative interpretations took on the aura of infallibility. Thus, the substantive law *(fiqh)* found in the manuals of the law schools, much of which was conditioned by historical and social circumstances as well as the use of reason, came to be "enshrined" as a detailed immutable blueprint for society. The doctrine of *taqlid* (imitation or following) was the natural conclusion to this process of the sacralization of tradition.

IJTIHAD VS. TAQLID

At the center of the struggle for reform is the doctrine of *taqlid*. According to this teaching, with the end of the period of the great *imams* (end of the tenth century), Islamic law has reached its completion. No longer were jurists considered capable of or permitted to exercise independent reasoning. The doors of *ijtihad* were closed and the creative activity during the golden age of Islamic jurisprudence came to an end. It was followed by what a noted Muslim jurist has called "the era of sterility,"[2] which has lasted to the present time.

This state of affairs continued for an extended period of time mainly because Islamic society remained relatively stable. Few social forces or individuals challenged the authority of *taqlid* or the medieval legal manuals. Among the noteworthy exceptions, however, was Ibn Taymiyah (d. 1328), the distinguished Hanbali jurist who claimed his own right of *ijtihad.* Others did not follow his lead until the advent of pre-modernist movements in the eighteenth century. Muhammad ibn Abd al-Wahhab in Arabia (d. 1792) and Shah Wali Allah of Delhi (d. 1762) rejected the blind following of medieval jurists and asserted their right to *ijtihad.* Their general plan was to renew the Muslim community by going back to the primary sources, the *Quran* and *Sunnah* of the Prophet. Their efforts provided a principal legacy to Muslim modernism in the late nineteenth and twentieth centuries.

The great Egyptian modernist Muhammad Abduh wrote in the late 1900's of the disease of *taqlid* which afflicted many Muslims.[3] Abduh often argued that Islam had freed Muslims from blind imitation and enjoined the reasoning of *ijtihad:*

> The *Quran* directs us, enjoining rational procedure and intellectual inquiry. . . . It forbids us to be slavishly credulous and for our stimulus points to the moral of peoples who simply followed their fathers with complacent satisfaction and were finally involved in an utter collapse of their beliefs and their own disappearance as a community. . . . It *(taqlid)* is a deceptive thing, and though it may be pardoned in an animal is scarcely seemly in man.[4]

A similar attitude toward the continued right to *ijtihad* was voiced by the Indian modernist Sayyid Ahmad Khan, and in the twentieth century by the most celebrated Muslim modernist of Pakistan, Muhammad Iqbal (1875–1938) when he wrote: "The closing of the door of *Ijtihad* is pure fiction suggested partly by the crystallization of legal thought in Islam, and partly by that intellectual laziness which, especially in the period of spiritual decay, turns great thinkers into idols."[5]

The influence of the doctrine of *taqlid* in legislative reform can be seen in the indirect and often inconsistent legal techniques employed by modern Egyptian jurists to provide a *taqlid* façade and thus avoid the charge of practicing *ijtihad.* In Pakistan, the direct assertion by the Marriage and Family Laws Commission of 1955 of its right to *ijtihad* resulted in a swift and strong reaction from the majority of the *ulama* and other conservative forces which contributed to the delay until 1961 of family law legislation.

THE DISTINCTION BETWEEN *SHARIAH* AND *FIQH*

Modern legislators' dependence upon *taqlid* is directly related to an important distinction, often blurred in modern times, between *Shariah* and *fiqh. Shariah* is the Divine Law while *fiqh* is the product of human understanding that has sought to interpret and apply the Divine Law in space and time. It is the confusion of this distinction between *Shariah* and *fiqh*, reinforced by the doctrine of *taqlid,* that has led to the overly sacrosanct attitude toward the *fiqh* of the ancestors. Early jurists acknowledged this distinction. An awareness of the profound difference between the perfection of the *Shariah* and the imperfection of man's comprehension of it was well-illustrated by the reluctance of many early jurists to accept the office of *qadi,* a judicial office that would make them responsible before God not only for the interpretation but also for the application of law.

THE *USUL AL-FIQH* (SOURCES OF LAW) AND ISLAMIC REFORM

The Quran

The primary textual sources of the law are the *Quran* and *Sunnah* and it is to these that reformers address themselves.

As the very word of God, the *Quran* is the fundamental textual source of the *Shariah*. Not a comprehensive legal manual but rather an ethico-religious revelation, its primary legal value is as the sourcebook of Islamic values: The *Holy Quran* is the God-made, sublime statement of the ought-to-be ... the *Holy Quran* contains a complete and perfect world-and-life view."[6] It is the source from which the specific regulations of substantive law (*furu al-fiqh*) are derived through human effort.

The primary area of concern in the relationship between the *Quran* and legal reform is exegesis. A distinctive emphasis which emerges in modernist writings is the necessity to get at the motive, intent, or purpose behind *Quranic* passages.[7] This approach reasserts the original influence of *Quranic* values in the early development of law and, as such, seeks to renew the process by which *Quranic* values were applied to newly-encountered social situations in the first centuries of Islamic legal history. The demands of a rapidly-changing society require once more, as in the formative period, substantive legal reforms to meet the needs of the Muslim family. Therefore, a clear grasp of the content of the Divine Will as expressed in the *Quran* and as applicable today is imperative. The fundamental questions facing Muslims today are those that confronted the early jurists: "What is the moral imperative which the *Holy Quran* had brought from God? How does it read when translated into the language of obligation pertinent to the concrete situations of real life?"[8]

The possibility of *Quranic* norms providing a complete basis of legal reform has also been recognized by a Western authority on Islamic law: "The *Quranic* precepts are in the nature of ethical norms—broad enough to support modern legal structures and capable of varying interpretations to meet the particular needs of time and place."[9]

The task of Muslim exegetes is a systematic study of the value system of the *Quran* and the hierarchization of its ethico-religious values.[10] This method would resolve the problem of *naskh* ("abrogation", the suppression of one *Shariah* rule by a later one where divergent regulations exist) as well as supply a reasonable explanation for the claim of the comprehensiveness of the *Quran*. Most importantly, it would provide a context within which one could understand the value of specific *Quranic* regulations.

Emphasis would be shifted beyond the specific regulations to its intent, to the value it sought to uphold.

Thus a *Quranic* prescription has two levels of importance — the specific injunction or command, whose details may be relative to its space and time context, and the ideal or *Quranic* value, whose realization the specific regulation intends to fulfill. Since the task of the Muslim community is the realization of these *Quranic* values, the goal of jurists is to insure that *fiqh* regulations embody these *Shariah* values as fully and perfectly as possible.

This approach could, for example, be applied to a particularly timely problem in family law reform, namely, the equality of the sexes. Verses from the *Quran* have been used by different factions to both support a woman's subservience to a man and to defend her rights of equality. This seeming contradiction can be resolved by an analysis of the relevant *Quranic* verses. One can reduce the concerns of these verses to two basic categories: the ethico-religious and the socioeconomic. On the ethico-religious level, the positions of men and women are on an equal standing, both as to their religious obligations toward God and their peers as well as their consequent reward or punishment: "The Believers, men and women, are protectors one of another: they enjoin what is just, and forbid what is evil; they observe regular prayers, practice regular charity, and obey God and His Apostle. On them will God pour His mercy.... God hath promised to believers men and women, gardens under which rivers flow, to dwell therein, and beautiful mansions to dwell in gardens of everlasting bliss" (IX:71–72).[11]

In the socioeconomic sphere, scholars of Islam agree that a major concern of the *Quran* was the betterment of woman's position by establishing her legal capacity, granting her economic rights (dower, inheritance, etc.), and thus raising her social status. However, some also cite *Quranic* verses whose traditional interpretations support what today would be an inequitable position for women. Perhaps the most commonly cited verse is *Quran* IV:34, which some interpret as indicating men's priority over women:[12] Men are in charge of women, because Allah hath made one to excel the other, and because they spend their property [for the support of women]."[13]

However, the "priority" attributed to men over women is

best understood as originating from their greater responsibility as protectors and maintainers within the socioeconomic context of Arabian society during the Prophet's time. Men, by virtue of their duty to defend and support their extended family members, enjoyed more rights and subsequently a different status in Muslim society. This understanding of man's role is illustrated by another possible translation of the same *Quranic* verse: "Men are the guardians [i.e. protectors and maintainers] over women because God made some of them [to excel] over others and because they [men] provide support from their wealth."[14]

The resolution of the dilemma caused by this verse in modern times can be found by applying the principle of the hierarchization of *Quranic* values.[15] The moral and religious equality of the sexes before God represents the highest expression of the value of equality. Furthermore, the ethico-religious equality of women is independent of, and not subject to, change of social situation. This value, then, enjoys a higher degree of priority over any value that is dependent upon a changing social context. The religious obligations incumbent upon man and woman equally belong to the *ibadat* (religious duties due God) regulations which are not subject to change. In contrast, matters of the socioeconomic sphere belong to *muamalat* (social relations, transactions) which are subject to change.

The assertion of man's "priority," in the sense of "responsibility" for woman, reflects his superiority over her by virtue of her socio-economic dependence upon him in a particular form of society. The traditional interpretation of man's priority mirrored the influence of customary practice upon some exegetes. However, when the social situation of women changes, as it has for increasing numbers of women in the twentieth century, they will no longer necessarily be dependent upon their husbands for maintenance and protection. Consequently, the concept of "priority" of husband over wife in the socioeconomic sphere is subject to change.

The two prime areas of family law affecting women's equal rights today are divorce and polygamy. Both provide excellent illustrations of the use of *Quranic* values in justifying legal reform.

As was noted in Chapter 2, while the Quran recognized

the necessity of divorce, it did so reluctantly, viewing divorce as a last resort where the marriage contract has been strained to its limits. The existence of these values in early Muslim society was further reflected in the traditions of the Prophet Muhammad, such as: "Get married, and do not divorce; indeed, divorce causes the Throne of God to shake!"[16]

The religious and social equality of women with men is a theme well-documented in the *Quran*. Equality is specifically affirmed in the area of divorce: "And women shall have rights similar to the rights against them, according to what is equitable" (II:228). While this verse recognizes equal rights of divorce for women, no *Quranic* verse supports the license of divorce presently awarded to males.

Equality of divorce rights is further exemplified in *hadith* literature. The *Sunnah* of the Prophet embodied in these *hadiths* provides a record of the Muslim community's lived experience of *Quranic* values. Where possible, then, while grounding legal changes in *Quranic* values, reformers can also utilize the traditions of the Prophet to ascertain how these values were understood and thus exemplified through the actions of the Prophet. One noteworthy tradition dealing with women's rights to dissolution is that of Aishah, the wife of the Prophet, who reported:

> A girl came and stated that her father had given her in marriage and told her to wait till the Prophet arrived. When the Prophet came, I told him the full story of the girl. He at once sent for the father of the girl and inquired of him whether the facts stated were true, after which he told the girl that she was at liberty to choose or repudiate her husband. The girl replied saying that she chose to retain her marriage, and that she wanted only to know whether women had any rights in the matter.[17]

The very form of this *hadith* reveals its didactic intent — that of affirming women's right of divorce. Another illustration of women's right to a dissolution of an unfavorable marriage is cited in a report from Imam Malik and Abu Daud. "The wife of Thabit bin Qais, Habibah bint Sahil . . . told the Prophet 'I and Thabit cannot pull together.' When Thabit came the Prophet said to him: 'This is what your wife says about you, so leave her.'"[18]

These *hadiths*, if coupled with the previously quoted *Quranic* teaching regarding women's right to divorce, provide an Islamic rationale for legal reform in divorce that will enjoy the twofold support of the traditionally-acknowledged material sources of Islamic law, the *Quran* and the *Sunnah* of the Prophet.

To implement this legal reform, citing the inequitable situation that has resulted from the male's abuse of *talaq* and basing oneself on *Quranic* values, a strong case can be made for establishing equal divorce rights by taking away the male's extra-judicial rights of repudiation and equalizing the option to exercise divorce by requiring that all divorce suits be subject to the courts as has been done in a number of Muslim countries.

In addition, based on *Quranic* values, arguments for the restriction and even the prohibition of polygamy are also possible. As was discussed in Chapter 2, the *Quran* had introduced reforms in pre-Islamic Arabian practice by restricting the prevalent practice and limiting the number of wives permitted a man to four. But even this permission was contingent upon the just treatment of each wife: "Marry women of your choice, two, three or four. But if ye fear ye shall not be able to deal justly (with them) then only one" (IV:3). Taking into consideration the unrestricted polygamy of pre-Islamic Arabia as well as the social situation in which this verse was written, namely the battle of Uhud and the death of many warriors and consequent problem of numerous widows and children[19] an argument could be made that the social context of these *Quranic* times made it difficult to go beyond the limitation of four wives. Yet one could conclude with Muhammad Abduh and Ahmad Khan that the ideal of the *Quran*, as seen in the *Quranic* value of impartiality, is monogamy.[20] Thus, the *Quranic* value of "equal justice" for each wife can be used as the criterion for restricting polygamy today. A similar approach has been used in drafting legal regulations which require a married man who wishes to take another wife to demonstrate to the courts his ability to treat his wives equally in terms of finances as well as love and affection.

Moving even further, the absolute prohibition of polygamy may be based on the requirement of impartiality and the impossibility of its full realization today. *Quranic* support for this contention is available. In addition to *Quran* IV:3, a corollary verse states: "Ye are never able to be fair and just as between women, even if it is your ardent desire" (IV:129). Therefore, an Islamic defense of the above legal changes in divorce and polygamy could be based upon the argument that a necessary continuation of the ongoing task of Muslim jurisprudence is to insure that the laws of *fiqh* for each age express *Quranic* values as fully as possible. Subhi Mahmasani in discussing the reasons for the decline of Muslims underscores the failure of some early jurists to incorporate *Quranic* values in law as fully as possible: "However some jurists were influenced by dominant pre-Islamic customs. . . and declined to apply in such cases the rulings imposed by the teachings of religion. If they had done so, giving religious and ethical principles more consideration, along with as much implementation in law as had been possible, their attitude would have been closer to the spirit of Islamic jurisprudence and teaching."[21] In effect, then, these reforms may be viewed as taking those *Quranic* values which traditionally had been regarded as moral exhortations for Muslims' personal conscience and incorporating them as legal conditions.

The *Sunnah* of the Prophet

As has already been indicated in examples of *hadiths* regarding marriage and divorce, an axiological approach can validly be applied to the second material source of law—the *Sunnah* of the Prophet. The *Sunnah* also provided those Islamic values which permeated the development of classical legal theory. To focus once more on these ideals, freeing them where necessary from the limitations of specific details which reflect the space and time context of early Islamic society, would enable the reapplication of these *Sunnah* values in contemporary Muslim society.

The validity of this method is justified by an appreciation of the historical development of *Sunnah* and *hadith*. Twentieth century scholarship has, in fact, demonstrated that the development of Islamic jurisprudence in general and *Sunnah* in particular was a much more dynamic and creative process than classical theory would suggest. Indeed, at the center of the creation of Muslim law by jurists and *qadis* was the application of Islamic values to the concrete social situations facing the community on a wider scale than had even been imagined. Thus, a more accurate historical view provides a corrective for misconceptions regarding the formation and nature of Islamic law. This results, as will be seen, in a rationale or methodology more conducive to Muslim family law reform, as well as Islamic reform in general.

Although the classical theory of *Sunnah* and *hadith*[22] has predominated until modern times, twentieth century Orientalist scholarship has rejected the authenticity of much of the Prophetic *Sunnah*. Drawing on the investigations of I. Goldziher, D. S. Margoliouth and C. S. Hurgronje,[23] Joseph Schacht in his *Origins of Muhammadan Jurisprudence* concluded that the bulk of the Prophetic *Sunnah* could not be considered authentic in the classical sense.[24] Schacht believed that very little information about the Prophet, outside of the *Quran*, was handed down from the past. He maintained that what is called *Sunnah* of the Prophet is not the words and deeds of the Prophet, but apocryphal material originating from customary practice that was back-projected in the eighth century to a more authoritative source: first the Successors, then the Companions, and finally to the Prophet himself.[25]

Schacht's thesis, then, is that the term *Sunnah* of the Prophet actually developed for the first time in the eighth century under the influence of the Traditionalist Movement and the aegis of al-Shafii was the first major jurist to limit the term *sunnah* (custom or practice) to the verified *Sunnah* of the Prophet, i.e., his model behavior. Schacht maintains that the use of this term actually gave legal authority to later customary practices and traditions. Therefore, he claims, what is called *Sunnah* of the Prophet is not a reliable source of Prophetic norms.

Schacht further held that because al-Shafii had won special status for the *Sunnah* of the Prophet as a material source of law, he had essentially excluded those traditions of the early schools that many believed were true manifestations of the Prophetic *Sunnah*. As a result, many jurists recognized the need to justify and authenticate those traditions they favored. Thus, the fifty-year period following Shafii's death witnessed a sudden burgeoning of narratives *(hadith)* about the Prophet's actions which came about in one of two ways: first, by the original creation of new *hadiths* which were actually contemporary interpretations of what the Prophet would have said or done about some problem, or, second, by the projection of *sunnahs* originating from the Companions or Successors back to the most authoritative source, the Prophet himself.[26] On the basis of his research, Schacht found no evidence of legal traditions before 722 or one hundred years after the death of the Prophet.

Although Schacht's findings are helpful for more fully understanding the creative role of the community in the development of Islamic law, his conclusions seem excessive. To state that no tradition goes back prior to 722 creates an unwarranted vacuum in Islamic history. To consider all *hadith* apocryphal until they are proven otherwise is to reverse the burden of proof. Rather, a *hadith* accepted for over ten centuries should stand until proven otherwise. This sifting process, while more laborious than Schacht's approach, seems sounder. Secondly, the "first century vacuum" theory does violence to the deeply ingrained sense of tradition in Arab culture which all scholars, both Muslim and Orientalist, have acknowledged. As Fazlur Rahman notes: "The Arabs, who memorized and handed down poetry of their poets, sayings of their soothsayers and statements of their judges and tribal leaders, cannot be expected to fail to notice and narrate deeds and sayings of one whom they acknowledged as the Prophet of God."[27]

And finally, what of the science of *hadith* verification with its specific and detailed criteria for establishing authority? While it was not foolproof and forgeries certainly existed, the wholesale inaccuracy that Schacht and those who follow him in this matter attribute to this Muslim science is unjustified.

The central problem that Schacht's thesis seems to have created for Islamic jurisprudence involves the normativeness of the *Sunnah*. Many Western scholars, on the basis of Schacht's findings, have maintained that the so-called "Prophetic *Sunnah*" are merely the attitudes of early generations of Muslims (actual customary practices) that developed normativeness only after two centuries when they were idealized as "*Sunnah* of the Prophet." Rather than constituting a stumbling block, the findings of Schacht, if correctly understood, present a dynamic picture of the development of Islamic law which demonstrates the viability of the sources of Muslim jurisprudence as a methodology for change.

Much of the misunderstanding about *Sunnah* results from

its long and various usage in history. The original meaning of the base root of the word, *sanna*, is "to open or pave a road, to introduce, or set an example." The secondary meaning is "to follow." *Sunnah* in the sense of first introducing a precedent and second following that precedent was used even in pre-Islamic times.

With the advent of Islam, while some pre-Islamic customs were rejected, most continued—some reformed, some supplemented, and others approved either expressly or tacitly. They could never again be merely the customs of pre-Islamic days because tribal practices and beliefs (i.e. customs) had been accepted or modified by the *Quran* and by the example of the Prophet. Muhammad's judgments, attitudes, and conduct revealed *Quranic* values in concrete form as he lived daily in the community. This concrete revelation set new precedents to be followed—the Prophetic *Sunnah*. These precedents were acted upon as future generations set their own examples or *sunnahs*. It is in this sense that Abu Yusuf in his *Kitab al-Kharaj* asks the Caliph Harun al-Rashid "to introduce some good *sunnahs*."[28] The values of the Prophetic *Sunnah* permeated early Muslim society both in themselves (i.e. Muslim works and deeds) and as ideals in light of which new practices were judged and either accepted or rejected.

But just how the reality of the *Sunnah* of the Prophet had been operating through the early generations must yet be described. As has been indicated, the term *"sunnah"* has been used throughout history to describe a number of phenomena. We have discussed the meanings or usages of the term *sunnah* as precedents established by the ancestors in pre-Islamic Arabia as well as the Prophetic *Sunnah* or Muhammad's ideal conduct that superseded and modified the pre-Islamic customs. This led to the *sunnah* or exemplary behavior of the earliest generations (the Companions) in the Islamic community, the behavior that grew out of the precedents set by the Prophet. To this list we must add the *sunnah* of the next generation, the Successors, which consisted of their interpretations of law based on the living tradition of the earlier generations and the *hadith*. The interpretations of early jurists in this period who reasoned on the basis of *Sunnah* varied. Disagreement about which incidents in the Prophet's life were more significant to a certain problem and their application naturally led to differing regional interpretations, and so regional *sunnah* developed. All, however, were ultimately based on Prophetic *Sunnah*.

A significant point to remember is that in early Islamic thought *Sunnah* of the Prophet was far from being differentiated from the *sunnahs* that followed: *sunnahs* of the Companions or of the Successors. People who believed that they were following the Islamic norm would naturally equate the Prophet's *Sunnah* with their own. For example, the early Medinese community viewed itself as the community of the Prophet, having lived directly under the Prophet and his Companions. Quite naturally, they would equate their way of life with the *Sunnah* of the Prophet and would never have occasion to draw distinctions.

Prophetic *Sunnah* served as the point of reference for Companions, and through their example, for the Successors who followed. The admissability of an action was judged in the light of the Prophetic ideal, *Sunnah* values. This understanding of Prophetic *Sunnah*, while it adds a more dynamic and creative dimension to the theory developed by medieval Muslim scholars, comes to the same conclusion in its emphasis on the importance of *Sunnah* as a material source of law. The normativeness of *Sunnah* as a source of Islamic values remains, while a more historical and developmental understanding emerges. The classical idea of *hadith* literature as bonafide narrative reports that convey the Prophet's *Sunnah* has been the subject of considerable controversy. Much of modern scholarship, following Schacht's theory regarding the development of *Sunnah*, has maintained that most, if not all, of the traditions ascribed to the Prophet were actually written much later, and therefore lack authenticity. But were the *hadith* always regarded as strictly historical? Many *hadiths* themselves seem to admit the formulation of new traditions. Consider, for example, the tradition in which the Prophet says: "Sayings attributed to me which agree with the *Quran* go back to me whether I actually said them or not," or the *hadith* in which the Prophet says, "Whatever of good saying there be, I can be taken to have said it.[29]

These *hadiths* and many others evidence concern not for strict historicity, but rather for sound interpretation of *Quranic* norms. In keeping with this line of thought, Fazlur Rahman calls the *hadith* "the *Sunnah-Ijtihad* of the first generations of Muslims,"[30] a "gigantic and monumental commentary of the Prophet by the early community" which "constitutes an epitome of the wisdom of Classical Muslims."[31]

Thus, despite the lack of historicity of some *hadiths,* they still represent the Prophet-directed vehicle for the interpretation and elaboration of *Quranic* norms. As such, they provide a rich source of Islamic values as lived and realized by the early community. As H. A. R. Gibb has observed: "Study of the *hadith* is not confined to determining how far it represents the authentic teaching and practice of Muhammad and the primitive Madinan community. It serves also as a mirror in which the growth and development of Islam as a way of life and of the larger Islamic community are most truly reflected.[32]

In conclusion, while the result of twentieth century critical studies does render an interpretation of the historical development of *Sunnah* which differs from the classical theory, this does not constitute a threat to Islam. Rather, a reinterpretation of the formation and nature of Islamic jurisprudence emerges. The result is a dynamic picture of the ongoing process of Islamization which is reflected in the *hadith* collections of the *Sunnah* of the Prophet. This same traditional methodology (as newly understood or rediscovered), contributes to a viable method for contemporary legal reform. That process which was essentially formulated to meet the needs of the classical period and was unfortunately "frozen" by the "closing of the door of *ijtihad*" and the ascendancy of *taqlid* (blind imitation), can now be continued once more.

Ijtihad

Ray and Qiyas

In addition to the two material sources of Islamic law, the *Quran* and *Sunnah,* the classical sources *(usul al-fiqh)* included *qiyas* (analogy) and *ijma* (consensus). As with the textual sources, the fuller historical perspective of *qiyas* and *ijma* available today enhances their viability as mechanisms for contemporary legal reform by showing their original dynamic nature.

Study of the development and usage of *qiyas* must be placed within the general context of the development of *ijtihad,* of which it is a part. *Ijtihad* means "self-exertion," to exert oneself in understanding and interpreting the *Shariah.* During the period of the early development of Islamic Law, the *ijtihad* was *ijtihad al-ray,* the exercise of "opinion or personal judgment" by the early *qadis* (judges).[33] The history of Islamic law shows that *ray* played an important role in the decisions of the early *qadis* and the functioning of the ancient schools of law. The task of the early *qadis* was the application of local law. Basing themselves on the customs of their locale as well as *Quranic* norms and available *Sunnah,* the *qadis* would render their opinion via legal decisions. The legal decisions of the courts were almost totally dependent upon the personal discretion of each *qadi* both as to his understanding of local law as well as the extent of his application of *Quranic* norms.

Ray also played an important role in the early development of the ancient schools of law during the eighth century; it was especially associated with the schools of Iraq.

The jurists of the early law schools employed *ray* in the formulation of new rules. Finding themselves a century after the Prophet in a socio-economic situation quite different from that of seventh century Arabia, the task of the Iraqis often involved the formulation of Islamic solutions for new problems. Reason was employed to extend divine prescriptions to novel situations. The use of personal judgment became progressively more systematic and disciplined by the use of *qiyas,* analogical reasoning.

Throughout the dynamic processes described above, the major activity which emerges is the use of reason to apply *Shariah* values derived from the *Quran* and *Sunnah.* These were a determining factor in *qadi* decisions, and most importantly, constituted the ultimate standard for the process of Islamization undertaken by the ancient schools of law. Furthermore, *Shariah* values continued to occupy a central role in the drafting of Islamic solutions for newly encountered problems: first, in the use of *ray* and even more consistently and systematically, with the development of *qiyas (ijtihad al-qiyas)* (reasoning by analogy). The role of *Shariah* values in the process of *qiyas* has aptly been described as: "The deduction, from a *shariah* principle, of the *hukm,* or *shariah* value, applicable to a new problem.[34]

Istislah

The use of reason, in fact, stretched beyond the *ijtihad al-qiyas*, which came to be the only form recognized by classical theory. For Islamic jurisprudence was concerned with insuring the *Quranic* concern for human welfare,[35] justice, and equity.[36] This concern to guarantee that should the letter of the law as arrived at through *qiyas* result in a harsh or rigid conclusion, a means be available to restore its spirit, resulted in the principles of *istishab* (presumption of continuity), *istihsan* (juristic preference), and *istislah* (public interest).[37] It is this last principle, *istislah*, which seems best suited for contemporary legal reforms for it provides a greater scope for the exercise of *ijtihad* and clearly puts into perspective the ends of law, namely, justice and equity, and human welfare or public interest *(maslahah)*.

The employment of the Maliki principle of *maslahah* as a source of contemporary legal reform was championed by Muhammad Abduh and his follower, Muhammad Rashid Rida[38] and the Salafiyyah movement, a reform movement initiated by Jamal al-Din al-Afghani (1839–1897) and carried on by Abduh and his disciple Rida.

The traditional Maliki position was that the *muamalat* (social transactions) regulations of the *Quran* and *Sunnah* had rational connotations and that God's purpose in revealing them was the promotion of human welfare. Thus, a jurist should select an interpretation which best accorded with the public interest *(maslahah)*.

Abduh and Rida extended this concept so that where social needs were not covered by specific *Shariah* texts, a jurist using his reason might interpret the law in light of the public interest. The result was a method *(istislah)* by which Islamic law might continuously and comprehensively be adapted to changing societal needs.

Istislah can function today in two instances: first, when conclusions arrived at through reasoning by analogy *(qiyas)* seem contrary to public interest; second, where a social need exists and the interest involved has not been covered by any specific *Shariah* texts. This latter usage is relevant in modern Muslim law reform. The introduction of legislation becomes possible provided such legislation is in the public interest and in harmony with the spirit of the *Shariah*, i.e., *Shariah* values. The result is a comprehensive methodology for reform which provides the recognition of the social welfare dimension of law as well as its Islamic character. While this approach differs somewhat from the classical formulation (law as the product of the *Quran* and *Sunnah* texts, analogical deductions, and consensus), it is, in fact, more in accord with the actual history of Islamic law in which historical and social influences and needs played important roles.

This use of *istislah* places greater emphasis on the probability of law rather than its infallibility. The greater recognition of the use of reason, in determining a more equitable solution in light of public interest and its concordance with *Shariah* values, underscores the human character and limitations of the substantive law of *fiqh*.

The employment of *istislah* as outlined above would resolve a juristic difficulty caused by the position advocated by the majority report of Pakistan's Marriage and Family Laws Commission in 1956.[39] The majority advocated a right to *ijtihad* provided the desired social change was not prohibited by the *Quran*. Such a methodology appeared to lack a positive Islamic rationale and thus seemed simply utilitarian and un-Islamic. However, the same results could be achieved by the advocacy of the principle of *istislah*. Its use would result in the more positive emphasis on looking to the revealed texts for *Shariah* values to support the legislation rather than the negative criterion of lack of *Quranic* injunction. A continuity between reform legislation and the Islamic tradition would be more clearly established. In addition, acceptance of the criterion of public welfare (*maslahah*) means recognition that should the interests of the community necessitate change, the law can adapt itself. This would assure the Islamic character of a dynamic and comprehensive law.

The Egyptian reform that sought to protect the rights of orphaned grandchildren of the deceased[40] provides a good illustration of the use of *istislah*. In drafting their reform legislation, Egyptian reformers took a circuitous route and avoided a direct change in the law of inheritance since they could find no traditional authority to ostensibly follow. Instead, they took an indirect route and provided for orphaned grandchildren by introducing the concept of "obligatory bequest" in the law of testamentary disposition.

However, a more direct reform in the law of inheritance itself could have been achieved by a twofold argument which satisifed the two criteria for the exercise of *istislah,* i.e., public welfare and consonance with the spirit of the *Quran.* First, the general welfare of Muslim society requires the rectification of this deficiency in the law of inheritance so that the rights of orphaned grandchildren are protected. Second, such a change is in harmony with the spirit of the *Quran* in which the welfare of orphans is a prominent theme.[41] In addition, the general intent of the *Quran* regarding inheritance is to protect inheritance rights, as witnessed by the "inheritance verses,"[42] and not to deprive someone of his share.

This same argument (i.e., the general welfare of Muslim society plus *Quranic* concern to protect inheritance rights) applies to the Egyptian reform regarding collaterals of the deceased. Through this reform, collaterals were protected by giving them a right of succession equivalent to that of the grandfather of the deceased. As has been discussed, this was done to prevent their exclusion from inheritance in their brother's or sister's estate by their uncle.[43]

Ijma

Because of its role in closing the door of *ijtihad, ijma* (consensus) has often been associated with the stagnation of *taqlid* (blind imitation). Such an understanding can be deceptive if *ijma* is understood as an unchanging Islamic institution from earliest times. In fact, the concept of *ijma* enjoyed a complex history of formulation, best characterized as a living creative process.

The earliest stage of *ijma* was that of the period immediately after the Prophet when almost every Muslim had been a "Companion" of the Prophet. During this time, *ijma* functioned not as a conscious concept but rather as the agreed-upon practice of the Muslim community living in accordance with the *Quran* and the example *(Sunnah)* of the Prophet. This same situation held true for the next two generations, that of the "Successors", i.e., the Companions' children *(tabiin)* and the Companions' children's children *(tabii al-tabiin).*

With the passage of time, the community grew and spread geographically. Muslims increasingly found themselves in differing social situations faced with many new problems. It was during this period that the early law schools developed and that *ijma* as a formal legal principle emerged.

Political and juristic leaders of the early communities in Medina, Iraq, Syria, etc., exercised *ijtihad* (interpretation) to determine new modes of action. The agreed-upon practice of these leaders constituted the *ijma al-aimmah*, i.e., the consensus of the leaders.

Early *ijma*, then, provided the Muslim community with a living instrument for revision and growth in the creation of fresh law to fit changing times. In the ancient schools of law, the relationship between *ijtihad* (interpretation) and *ijma* (consensus) was an ongoing process, moving from individual opinion to community approval to accepted practice to difference of opinion if conditions changed, and therefore to the reinterpretation of *ijtihad* and *ijma* again.

Moreover, this process of thinking and re-thinking was itself subject to differing views as to its nature. Early in its development, *ijma* was more a regional interpretation by the jurists of a particular province. The Maliki School, for example, gave great emphasis to the *ijma* of Medina. Since it was the home of the Prophet, they felt that their *ijma* was a continuation of the Prophet's *Sunnah*. The Hanbalis stressed the *ijma* of the Companions. The Shafii and Hanafi Schools believed that *ijma* should be applied not only to the earliest generations but to all times and to all geographical areas.

Ijma contributed to the great diversity of interpretation and doctrine in the Muslim community, a diversity which, as we have seen, clashed with the strong Traditionist Movement *(Ahl al-Hadith)* in the eighth century, with its successful drive for uniformity both in the sources of law and therefore, in substantive law itself. The *ijma* practiced by the early schools was strongly condemned by al-Shafii for its diversity. He recognized only the consensus of the entire Muslim community as valid and thus insistently told the differing schools, "You do not have agreement *(ijma)* but disagreement *(iftiraq)*." Al-Shafii's conception of *ijma* was radically different from that of the early schools. For them, *ijma* was not al-Shafii's theoretical and, practically speaking, unworkable source of law which required a total agreement of all Muslims. The *ijma* of the early schools, linked as it was with *ijtihad* in a dynamic dialectical process, provided a powerful means for the adaptation of law to changing circumstances. But with the increasing power of the *Ahl al-Hadith* and the consequent rejection of original interpretations of the law through *ijtihad,* the organic interrelationship between *ijtihad* and *ijma* was severed. *Ijma* was isolated—no longer in dynamic tension with fresh *ijtihad,* it became a principle of rigid approval which, once made, was considered forever binding.

In the final classical theory of Islamic law, established in the tenth century, the agreed-upon doctrines of the schools were considered fixed, unchangeable. Henceforth, jurists were to practice *taqlid,* to follow the established principles of their individual schools. Thus the "closing of the door of *ijtihad*" in the medieval period, which had its authoritative basis in the consensus of the scholars of the time, became the prime cause for the general loss of dynamism.

Al-Ghazzali (d. 1111) was among the noteworthy exceptions in this process of legal stagnation. He recognized the consensus of the religious scholar *(ijma al-ulama)* of a generation as a source of law and thus continued to acknowledge the possibility of a living consensus. However, the process of legal stagnation was not to be reversed.

Modernist Muslim thought has sought to restore *ijma* to its rightful place and thus re-establish the dynamic dialectic of the *ijtihad-ijma* relationship. Muhammad Abduh, the "Father of Muslim Modernism," who was a strong advocate of the role of reason, the right of *ijtihad,* viewed *ijma* as a consensus of reason which can reasonably be presumed free from error.[44] However, Abduh's concept of *ijma* is less dogmatic than the traditional notion. His idea of freedom from error is more the presumption of a reasonable possibility, where the agreement of a generation's most learned interpreters *(mujtahidun)* is obtained, than the affirmation of an absolute infallibility.[45] Abduh recognized the right of future generations, in view of changed circumstances, to reinterpret the law *(fiqh).* In this way, the dynamic relationship between reason *(ijtihad)* and collective reason or a consensus of reason *(ijma)* is restored.

Muslim modernists follow Abduh's position *vis á vis ijma* and the question of its infallibility. In essence, no denial of the value and binding power of *ijma* occurs relative to the period in which it occurred. For indeed, the function of *ijma* is to serve as a brake and safeguard on individual subjective *ijtihad,* which by itself is no more than fallible conjecture *(zann),* and either to reject it as erroneous or to approve it as applicable for Muslim society. What modernists reject is an unlimited or absolute infallibility which denies that such as *ijma* is open to question and change in future generations as societal circumstances change.[46]

Among reformers in the Indian subcontinent, a progressive reinterpretation of *ijma* has occurred in an attempt to adapt it to the needs of contemporary Muslim society. Ameer Ali (1849–1928) advocated the broadening of the notion of *ijma* and its incorporation within the constitutional government of a modern state.[47] This general notion has become progressively more developed in the writings of Muslim reformers such as Muhammad Iqbal (1875–1938), considered by many to be the outstanding twentieth century modernist of India-Pakistan, and Fazlur Rahman.

Iqbal described *ijma* as "perhaps the most important legal notion in Islam."[48] He recommended the transferral of *ijtihad* "from individual representatives of schools to a Muslim legislative assembly."[49] The *ijma* of the community would be equated with the consensus of the legislatures of modern Muslim states.

Fazlur Rahman, former director of Pakistan's Islamic Research Institute and a member of the Islamic Ideology Council, has pursued a similar line of argument. For Rahman, the *Quran* is not a law book, but rather a guide. Within the framework of its general moral principles the Islamic community is free to develop its legal system. Even those "quasi-laws as do occur in the *Quran* are not meant to be literally applied in all times and climes; the principles on which these legal or quasi-legal pronouncements rest have to be given fresh embodiments in legislative terms."[50] As with most Muslim modernists, Rahman's methodology rests on the dual principles of *ijtihad* and *ijma* which provide both the dynamism and permanence required to meet the needs of a changing society. *Ijtihad* is that means by which individuals "think out new solutions of problems on the basis of Islamic principles."[51] The

Islamic community will then have a spectrum of interpretations to weigh, discuss, and debate. The consensus which emerges from this process is its *ijma*, that consensus which will inform new laws passed by the legislature. Should public opinion change, the law is repealed and replaced by one which embodies the new consensus of the community *(ijma)*.

What emerges from the equation of *ijma* with the consensus of a modern legislative assembly is a reinterpretation which is significantly different from traditional usage. In the past, the consensus of the community as a whole *(ummah)* or of the major figures in the law schools *(imams)* or of the religious scholars *(ulama)* occurred over a protracted period of time as certain interpretations *(ijtihad)* became more accepted than others and eventually became the agreed-upon practice. This traditional view of consensus is quite different from that obtained through the process of legislation in a national assembly.

Effective change need not necessitate the reorientation of *ijma* advocated by Iqbal and Rahman. Their suggestions regarding the transfer of *ijtihad* to a legislature can be used productively for dynamic legal changes to meet societal needs. At the same time, the difficulties which their method raises can be circumvented by equating the resulting social legislation with *ijtihad* alone and not *ijma*.

It is at this point that the dynamic relationship of *ijtihad* and *ijma* can be restored. *Ijma* provides the test of time and community experience which a new interpretation *(ijtihad)* must undergo in order that its long-range value be accepted by the community. If the new legislation *(ijtihad)* does not survive the questioning and debate within the community, it will be repealed and replaced. In contrast, should it remain unchanged, then its community acceptance *(ijma)* and authority will be established. However, it is important to note that even this fresh *ijma* may in future generations be subject to renewed *ijtihad* as the dialectical process continues.

An illustration will serve to clarify this process and its importance. The question of polygamy has been a major issue in twentieth century Muslim family law reform. Reformers in most Muslim countries have attempted to restrict the exercise of polygamy through legislation based on their interpretation of *Quranic* values which concludes that monogamy is the *Quranic* ideal and thus should be the community's legal norm. The reform called for would constitute a significant departure from traditional Muslim social and legal practice. Furthermore, it means serious change affecting husbands, wives, and children. Therefore, the acceptance of monogamy as a long-range religious norm must be approached cautiously. To equate a legislative change enacted at a particular point in history by a single act of a legislative group with the *ijma* of the community is a drastic step. The passage of such legislation may be due to fortuitous circumstances in which a strong minority legislates a position repugnant to the majority. Such reform legislation may be repealed soon afterwards, or simply ignored by the majority of the population. Equating such an activity with *ijma* would reduce it to a meaningless concept.

Historically, it is possible to view the question of polygamy vis à vis monogamy in the contemporary Muslim world as a juncture in the *ijtihad-ijma* dialectic. Throughout the twentieth century, reformers have called for change. Initial draft legislation such as that submitted to and approved by the Egyptian Cabinet in 1927 was vetoed by King Fuad. However, in 1953 *Article 17* of the *Syrian Law of Personal Status* enacted the first law restricting polygamy. Since then other countries such as Pakistan have passed similar legislation. The most sweeping legislation occurred in 1957 when *Article 18* of the *Tunisian Law of Personal Status* decreed that polygamy was prohibited.

The debate regarding polygamy in the Muslim world today continues. Personal as well as collective (legislative) *ijtihad* has offered two basic reform positions—restriction of polygamy or prohibition of polygamy. These are juxtaposed against the traditional *ijma* supporting the right of polygamy. Out of this protracted debate, a new *ijma* will emerge.

The use of *ijtihad* and *ijma* to provide a rationale for drafting Islamic law raises two controversial issues: (1) Who possesses the power to make laws? and (2) What is the role of the *ulama* (religious scholars)? Many conservative Muslims would agree that only Allah (God) can make laws and, thus, no individual or elected body can legislate. Most of the *ulama* and their followers would claim that only the *ulama* possess the traditionally accepted qualifications and expertise required to be a *mujtahid* (one who exercises the right of *ijtihad*).

The dispute regarding the power to make laws is again

rooted in a failure to distinguish between the immutable *Shariah* (the divinely revealed principles and values) and *fiqh* (that body of law worked out by jurists and therefore the product of human understanding, interpretation, and application) which is historically conditioned and subject to change. Due to the predominance of the doctrine of *taqlid,* the law enshrined in the legal manuals has been viewed in practice if not in theory as divinely mandated. Thus, even where conservative religious leaders speak of the possibility of changing certain *fiqh* regulations, in practice they are often loath to do so.

The second issue — who is qualified to interpret Islamic law — is rooted in the *ulama's* assertion of their traditional role as guardians of the law. They claim that they alone possess the traditionally accepted qualifications of a *mujtahid* (interpreter). Muslim reformers respond that the term *alim* (pl. *ulama*) simply means a learned person. Since there is no ordained clergy in Islam, all Muslims may qualify for this designation. As to the areas of knowledge which a *mujtahid* must possess, reformers maintain that knowledge of the traditional religious disciplines *(Quran, hadith, Shariah)* is not restricted to the *ulama.* More importantly, the demands of modernity are such that expertise in many modern disciplines, such as economics, psychology, and sociology are also required today. This expertise falls beyond the competence of most *ulama.* Indeed the *ulama* are looked upon by many reformers as obstacles to change—men whose limited training and world view, as well as a tendency to protect their own vested interests, prevent them from fully appreciating the demands of modernity and providing the leadership necessary for Islamic reform. The Iranian reformer Ali Shariati noted that the traditional religious leaders "suppressed true knowledge of religion, and hindered the true understanding of Shii beliefs."[52]

Custom[53]

In seeking an Islamic rationale for contemporary legal reforms, besides the official sources of Islamic jurisprudence, there are "extraneous sources" (from the classical viewpoint) which contributed significantly to substantive law. By far the most important of these is customary practice. A study of the role of custom provides a fuller picture of the sources of the material content of law and helps to explain the existence of certain attitudes and mores evident in classical family law.

Although not officially and theoretically recognized, customary law played a key role in the development of Islamic law. Custom *(adah, urf)* in pre-Islamic Arabia, as in many early traditional societies, served as law. For the majority of the Arabs, custom, the body of unwritten rules which had been developed and passed down through the generations, provided the positive laws of their society. Normative legal custom constituted the *sunnah* (path or way) of the tribe.

The advent of Islam signaled a profound and radical change in Arabian society. Yet, while recognizing the introduction of new beliefs, regulations, and institutions, a good deal of the Islamic way consisted of a reform of existing customs and a continuance of that which was not in need of specific reform.

There are numerous ways in which custom became incorporated into Islamic law, among them, the procedures of the *qadis* (judges), the content of traditions *(hadith)*, the Malikite regard for the *ijma* of Medina, and the *fatwas* of the *muftis*.

As noted previously, in the early courts of the Umayyad and early Abbasid periods, *qadis* in rendering a decision would look to the *Quran* and *Sunnah* for guidance, but where no relevant texts were found, they would then resort to the custom of their community. An example from the sphere of family law is the division of dower *(mahr)*. The practice was to separate the dower into two parts, the first paid immediately, and the other deferred usually until the ending of the marriage. In situations in which the proportionate amounts had not been stipulated in the contract, the allotment was usually determined on the basis of local custom. This approach continued to be followed in modern times. The *Majallah*[54] *(Ottoman Civil Code)* states: "A thing acknowledged by custom is regarded as an agreed upon stipulation" *(Article 43)*.

A second avenue for the entrance of custom into Islamic law was the tradition *(hadith)* literature. The usual classification of the *Sunnah* is *al-sunnah al-qawliyah* (words), *al-sunnah al-filiyah* (deeds), and *al-sunnah al-taqririyah* (what Muhammad permitted). It is this last category, comprising actions performed in the presence of the Prophet without his disapproval, which represents that body of pre-Islamic Arabian customary practice which continued to be followed.

The *ijma* (consensus) of the Maliki law school, which was restricted to that of the Medinan community, is indicative of another historical source for custom. Where no explit text existed, the customs of the Medinese were regarded as a legal source. Besides the importance of the Prophet's community, this Maliki concept reflects the early tendency for the *ijma* to be a local geographical consensus (for example, the *ijma* of Kufa, Basra, Medina) which became its *sunnah*, or ideal pattern of behavior of each local school. For example, the Hanafi doctrine of marriage equality *(kafaah)* which required that the husband be the equal of his wife in a number of respects, among them lineage, financial standing, and profession, is peculiar to the Hanafi school and reflects the practice of a more socially-stratified, class conscious society than Medina.

A final source for the incorporation of custom in law was the *fatwas* (opinions) of *muftis* (legal consultants). A *fatwa* is an opinion on a point of law rendered by a *mufti* in response to a question submitted to him by a private individual or by a *qadi*. The need for the office of *mufti* existed from the earliest period of legal development. Due to the vast expansion of Islam, the Islamic community found itself mingling with new cultures, novel ideas, and new problems. There were myriad occasions necessitating reference to competent legal scholars. As law developed and became increasingly complex, these legal specialists became increasingly important. Where a specific revealed text did not provide an answer to the legal problem before them, *muftis* adopted or modified customs of the day in light of *Shariah* values. As the times and their customs changed, so too might the substance of the *fatwa*.

Although the function of the *mufti* was essentially private and consultative, and so a *fatwa* was not legally binding, it could be utilized by a *qadi* and incorporated in his decision. More importantly, when a *fatwa* issued by a *mufti* on a new problem became recognized by the *ijma* of the scholars of a school, it was incorporated in the legal handbooks of the school. Finally, compilations of the responses of noted *muftis*, such as the *Fatawa*

Alamgiriyya, came to be reckoned among the important authoritative legal references complimenting the standard *Shariah* manuals.

Although not officially recognized by classical theory, customary practice, then, came to form a substantial part of Islamic law. This realization should assist reformers in three ways. First, it underscores the extent to which custom did contribute to the body of substantive law, and so the inclusion of modern social standards or customs can be viewed as consistent with the manner in which law had been formulated to meet particular social needs in the past. Second, it demonstrates the process of Islamization of this customary law and therefore lays the foundation and provides the method for the replacing of old customs with newly Islamized customs appropriate to changed social situations. Third, it emphasizes the extent to which *fiqh* was influenced by fallible and mutable human understanding both in its content (since custom is the non-revelational product of a human society) and method (the reason of the *qadis, muftis,* and jurists of the law schools whose decisions incorporated custom in law). This makes the distinction between *Shariah* and *fiqh* that much clearer to all who still do not distinguish the immutable and the sacrosanct in Islamic law from the fallible, the particular and the human.

CONCLUSION

The twentieth century represents a period in Islamic history as critical as any yet encountered. The central problem is modernization and the key question, change. Muslim family law reform provides the major arena for Islamic reform. Muslims have grappled with the two major issues of reform: (1) the relationship of tradition and change, and (2) the means or methodology for reinterpretation and reform.

The classical theory of law presented a definitive picture of the formation of law, both its jurisprudential method *(usul al-fiqh)* and the branches of substantive law themselves *(furu al-fiqh)*. The four sources of law *(Quran, Sunnah, qiyas,* and *ijma)* produced a body of law consisting of religious observances (*ibadat*) and social transactions (*muamalat*) of which family law is a major part. By the end of the tenth century the consensus (*ijma*) of scholars concluded that the basic rules of law had been discerned. The task of future jurists was to follow the teachings of the great *Imams* of the past. Thus, the gate of *ijtihad*, of independent interpretation, was closed, and *taqlid* or imitation reigned. Down through the ages, with few exceptions, the consensus of medieval jurists affirmed the completeness and authoritativeness for all times of law (*fiqh*) as found in the law books of the four Sunni schools. The law was complete; there was no need for substantive change.

As long as the structure of Muslim society remained essentially unchanged, Islamic law could generally meet the needs of the times. This is especially evident in the field of family law which remained operative until contemporary times. Muslim family law was a well-developed comprehensive approach to the major aspects of family life—marriage, divorce, inheritance, etc., basically in tune with medieval Muslim society. Thus, during the long span of ten centuries, the classical view of law reigned throughout Muslim society.

However, this situation has been abruptly challenged in the modern period as Muslim societies have sought to respond to the challenges of modernization. The results of these new developments have led to social changes, among them changes in family structure and most especially in woman's status and role in society. While these changes have not affected all of society to the same degree, reforms in Muslim family law have occurred in most Muslim countries.

Despite the changes thus far, the conflict between the forces of conservatism and modernism has continued. Resistance to change often resulted in indirect, ad hoc legal methods of reform as well as the shelving of draft legislation. The problem which has emerged is still very much that of *taqlid* (following tradition) versus *ijtihad* (reinterpretation), the infallibility of classical law versus legal change. The task is not an easy one, namely, to provide an Islamic rationale for change, one clearly rooted in Islamic history.

The importance of providing an Islamic methodology for Islamic reform is especially evident today. As noted at the outset of this study, one aspect of the Islamic renewal or resurgence is a call for more Islamically oriented societies. Given the totality of Islam and the comprehensiveness of its worldview as reflected in Islamic law, this has meant a call for more *Shariah* law. Potentially, such change could affect every area of life, from the nature and institutions of the state to family relations. Debates on the advisability of such attempts, as well as the nature of a return to *Shariah* rule, have occurred from Egypt and the Sudan to Pakistan and Malaysia. Does a return to *Shariah* law mean simply going back to those laws which developed during the first centuries of Islam and reflect the society of those times, or will it be a law which is the product of reinterpretation *(ijtihad)* and reform? As Muslims seek to root their personal and national identity in an Islamic past, the importance of reinterpretation *(ijtihad)* and community consensus *(ijma)* is evident. Providing an Islamic methodology for reform is an essential part of this process. Lack of such a methodology undermines any sense of the Islamic character of reforms and consequently the acceptance of such reforms by the vast majority of Muslims. While passage of reforms may be effected through an autocratic leader of a legislature comprised of a small elite, their ultimate acceptance by the vast majority of the Islamic community will not be assured. Thus, for example, the Islamic Republic of Iran has repealed the *Family Protection Act*. Pakistan is reviewing provisions of the *Muslim Family Laws Ordinance of 1961* which rests on a weak Islamic methodology. In Egypt, among the major criticisms levelled against the family law reforms of 1979 by conservatives was its questionable Islamic methodology which included the use of *talfiq*. Therefore, care in the mechanisms employed in rendering reforms is of the utmost importance. Islamic jurisprudence provides the resources for such an undertaking.

Contemporary scholarship has begun to provide the historical perspective and materials for such a project. The complex origins of Islamic law, long forgotten by the idealized traditional picture of classical theory, have resurfaced and, if properly interpreted, provide a historical justification for Muslim family law reform. More importantly, a new understanding of law's development demonstrates that Islamic jurisprudence is fully capable of again providing the methods for reform.

To once more realize the divine imperative in history, the

Muslim community possesses its immutable source—the *Quran*. Constant and firm belief that this sourcebook of Islamic values is the very revealed word of God provides Muslims with the principles and values upon which to base legal reform. If *Quranic* values are applied correctly, Muslim society can accommodate social change in the twentieth century while preserving its link with the history of the Islamic tradition. Furthermore, the task of reassessing the role of the *Sunnah* and its utilization in legal reform will not be a novel endeavor. Voices calling for a historical critique and re-evaluation of the *hadith* have existed throughout Islamic history from the early movement which led to the development of the science of hadith criticism to pre-modern reformers like Muhammad ibn Abd al-Wahhab and Shah Wali Allah and finally to the Muslim modernists of the twentieth century.[55]

However, the successful implementation of the last two sources of legal reform *(ijtihad* and *ijma)* constitutes the greatest challenge for contemporary Muslim society. Education continues to be the most important ingredient for change, for Islamic reform in general and women's status in particular. The basic fight against illiteracy as well as the struggle to reform the educational systems of both secular and religious institutions is essential. An important task in educational reform is the implementation of measures which insure that the educational system incorporates the best of both scientific knowledge and religious values.

Part of the legacy of modernity is the bifurcation of education in most Muslim countries through the creation of modern (national) schools alongside traditional (Islamic) schools — each with a curriculum reflecting differing and competing world views.[56] The situation has been further compounded in those Muslim countries where the government has sharply curtailed direct financial support for Islamic schools as well as reduced their revenue through the reform or repeal of religious endowments *(waqfs)*. The result of such a bifurcated educational system may be seen in its products. Western educated elites possess modern scientific and technological skills, but have little intellectual knowledge of or appreciation for their tradition. Therefore, they lack the vision to draft reforms which take into account the history and values of their culture. Traditionally educated individuals are the products not only of a limited curriculum which provides a deficient appreciation of modern problems, but one whose intellectual outlook does not incorporate a sense of the creative, dynamic process which characterized the formative period of Islam. Thus, they are less open to substantive reinterpretation and reform. As Fazlur Rahman has observed regarding the traditional Islamic schools (madrasa): "The madrasas have ... aimed at merely imparting a system of ideas not at creating newer systems; and therefore they have not been interested in inculcating the spirit of inquiry and independent thought."[57]

Education is a key factor in assuring the expertise necessary for a wise reinterpretation (ijtihad) and an enlightened community consensus (ijma) which keeps pace with social change.

The Islamic revival has highlighted not only the strength of traditional religious leaders and the force of the classical Islamic world view, but also the existence of a growing generation of Islamic reformers. In general, these reformers are not members of the ulama; many are Western educated but Islamically oriented. Alongside the Ayatullah Khumayni and the majority of Iranian religious leaders, the Islamic movement in Iran has included others like the sociologist Ali Shariati, and the economist and former Iranian president Abol Hasan Bani Sadr, both Sorbonne educated.[58] The more vibrant leaders of the Islamic movement in Malaysia are Western-educated professors and students.[59] Likewise, among the leaders of the Islamic movement in the Sudan are the Oxford-educated former Prime Minister, Sadiq al-Mahdi, and the London-Sorbonne educated Hassan Turabi, currently Attorney General of the Sudan as well as the President of the Muslim Brotherhood Party.

While differences abound, these Islamic reformers do share certain common attitudes. First, there is an acceptance of modernization, but a rejection of an uncritical adoption of westernization and secularization. Second, there is general agreement that more indigenously (Islamically) oriented models of political, economic, and social change need to be implemented. Third, reformers claim the right to ijtihad and thus reject a blind following of the past. Fourth, their methodology includes a return to fundamentals (in this sense they may truly be termed fundamentalists!), i.e., to the Quran and the example of the Prophet. While reverencing past tradition, they do not feel bound to it, since they view the traditional world view embodied in Islamic law as the product of past *ijtihad* to meet historically conditioned needs. Therefore, they see themselves as undertaking once again the process of Islamization which characterized the early formative period of Islam—a process during which Muslims borrowed freely from other cultures, adopted and adapted the best that was available, and added their own distinctive contributions. Once again, reformers seek to interpret and apply Islamic principles and values to the exigencies of modern life and thus develop appropriate Islamically acceptable responses for modern Muslim societies.

The challenges facing the developing nations of the Islamic world are formidable. What path(s) Muslim countries will ultimately choose is an open ended question. For many a present and future which embodies some continuity with their Islamic past will continue to be an important concern. Given the traditional role of Islamic law as the ideal, comprehensive statement of the Islamic way of life, calls for more *Shariah* reform are inevitable. Moreover, as Muslim women's status changes due to increasing educational and employment opportunities, pressures for continued family law reform will intensify.

Islamic history, if correctly understood, has a lesson for both conservatives and reformers. It offers a picture of a dynamic, changing, adaptive religious tradition. A fuller appreciation of the real as well idealized Islamic past can provide the understanding and means or methodology for Islamic responses to the challenge of modernity as Muslims once more repeat the process of Islamization—to develop a viable political, legal, and economic model for society and to draw on all available data and practices, but to do so in light of *Quranic* principles and values.

NOTES

PREFACE

1. John L. Esposito, ed., *Islam and Development: Religion and Sociopolitical Change* (Syracuse, N.Y.: Syracuse University Press, 1980).

1—THE SOURCES OF ISLAMIC LAW

1. "To Him is due the primal origin of the heavens and the earth; When He decreeth a matter, He saith to it: 'Be', and it is" *(Quran* II:117); see also *Quran* VII:54 and XXXI:10. All *Quranic* references are from *The Holy Quran, Text, Translation, and Commentary,* Abdullah Yusuf Ali, ed., (Beirut: Dar al-Arabia, 1968).

2. The scope of this study is restricted to Sunni Islam, that branch of Islam which encompasses 90 percent of the world's Muslims.

3. Shihab al-Din al-Qarafi, *Adh Dhakhira* (Cairo: 1961) 1:119. See also Muhammad ibn Idris al-Shafii *Al-Risala fi usul al-fiqh* (Cairo: Bulak, 1321 A.H.), pp. 65–66.

4. N. J. Coulson, *A History of Islamic Law* (Edinburgh: University of Edinburgh Press, 1964), p. 40.

5. Reuben Levy, *The Social Structure of Islam* (Cambridge: Cambridge University Press, 1971), p. 127.

135

2—CLASSICAL MUSLIM FAMILY LAW

1. W. Robertson Smith in his study *Kinship and Marriage in Early Arabia* (Boston: Beacon Press, 1903), p. 92, applied the Old Testament term for a husband *ba'al* (lord, owner or master) to describe such marriages. See also Reuben Levy, *The Social Structure of Islam* (Cambridge: Cambridge University Press, 1957), pp. 91 ff.

2. See also *Quran* VI:151 and XVII:31.

3. Charles Hamilton, trans., *The Hedaya* (Lahore: Premier Book House, 1957), p. 530.

4. Ibid., p. 37.

5. Sir D. F. Mulla, *Principles of Mahomedan Law*, 16th ed. (Bombay: Tripathi, 1968), p. 263.

6. See Hamudah Abd al-Ati, *The Family Structure In Islam* (Ann Arbor: University Microfilm, 1971), pp. 253–60 for a discussion of the religious, sociological, and psychological reasons for this prohibition.

7. How high soever (h.h s.) and how low soever (h.l.s.) refer to continuing the same family line as far as conceivable. For example, a son h.l.s. can refer to a son's son's son's son. A grandfather h.h.s. can refer to a father's father's father's father.

8. Neil B. E. Baillie, *A Digest of Moohummudan Law*, 4th ed. (Lahore: Premier Book House, 1965), p. 35.

9. Seymour Vesey-Fitzgerald, *Muhammadan Law: An Abridgement* (London: Oxford University Press, 1931), pp. 96–98.

10. Coulson, *A History of Islamic Law*, p. 175.

11. Faiz Badruddin Tyabji, *Muhammadan Law: The Personal Law of Muslims*, 3rd ed. (Bombay: Tripathi, 1940), pp. 264–65.

12. Hamilton, *The Hedaya*, p. 73.

13. See, for example, *Quran* LXV:1.

14. Vesey-Fitzgerald, *Muhammadan Law*, p. 73.

15. Two other forms of divorce initiated by the husband are very rare: *Ila* and *Zihar*. With *Ila* or Vow of Continence the husband vows not to have intercourse with his wife, and if he abstains for four months, in Hanafi law, the marriage is dissolved without legal process. However, he may revoke the vow by merely resuming marital life.

Zihar is derived from *zahr*, back. It is an archaic form of an oath coming from pre-Islamic Arabia. *Zihar* means "to oppose back to back," which represents dissension between husband and wife who each turn their back on the other partner. In the language of law, *zihar* signifies a husband comparing his wife to a female relative within the prohibited degrees of kinship. *Zihar* by itself does not dissolve the marriage. After the husband has taken this oath, his wife has the right to file for restitution of conjugal rights.

16. See Chapter 3, p. 81.

17. Tyabji, *Muhammadan Law*, pp. 275–76.

18. For additional information, see Baillie, *Digest*, pp. 696–700; Tyabji, *Muhammadan Law*, pp. 839, 843–60; Mulla, *Principles*, pp. 58–62. N. J. Coulson, *Succession in the Muslim Family* Cambridge: Cambridge University Press, 1971), pp. 40–46.

19. *The Sirajiyyah* by Siraju al-din Md. b. Abdu al-Rashid al-Sajawandi is the highest authority on inheritance among the Hanafis.

20. *Sirajiyyah*, 23–24, as cited in A. A. A. Fyzee, *Outlines of Muhammadan Law*, 3rd ed. (London: Oxford University Press, 1964), p. 411.

21. See also *Quran* II:240, which prescribes that a testator bequeath one year's maintenance with residence to his widow.

22. See Chapter 3, p. 65.

23. *Mishkat al-Masabih 12:xx, 1.*

24. *Ibid.* 12:xx, 2.

25. Baillie, *Digest*, p. 557.

3—MODERN MUSLIM FAMILY LAW REFORM IN EGYPT AND PAKISTAN

1. *Commercial Code of 1850, Penal Code of 1858, Code of Commercial Procedure of 1861*, and *Code of Maritime Commerce of 1863*.

2. Although the majority of Egyptians were followers of the Shafii school, the Hanafi school has been the authoritative source of the courts since the sixteenth century when the Ottoman Empire established it as the official law school. This action was reaffirmed by Article 280 of *Shariah Courts Organization Regulations, 1910*, in which predominant opinions of the Hanafi school were officially endorsed.

3. *Al-Manar*, 35 vols. (Cairo: Manar Press, 1912) 12:331.

4. Muhammad Abduh and Muhammad Rashid Rida, *Tafsir al-Qur'an al-Hakim*, 12 vols. (Cairo: Manar Press, 1349/1930) 4:349 ff.

5. Qasim Amin, *Tahrir al-Mar'ah (Cairo: n.p., 1899), pp. 165 and 184.*

6. *Quoted in C. C. Adams, Islam and Modernism in Egypt* (Oxford: Oxford University Press, 1933), p. 231.

7. J. N. D. Anderson, "Recent Developments in Shariah Law III," *Muslim World* 41 (1951): 113.

8. See Chapter 2, p. 35.

9. See Chapter 2, p. 17.

10. See Chapter 2, p. 36.

11. This provision requiring payment of past maintenance was the cause of many false claims as to the arrears date. The Code of 1931 decreed that claims could not be in excess of three years prior to the date of the suit.

12. *Articles 15 and 17, Law No. 25, 1929.*

13. See Chapter 2, pp. 37–38.

14. While the other Sunni schools of law do not allow dissolution of marriage, they each recommend other methods for handling cases of maltreatment.

15. *Article 9, Law No. 25, 1929.* While this legislation is principally of Maliki origin, one significant difference exists. Whereas the Maliki school allows for a *khul* divorce when the wife is judged at fault, the reform legislation makes no provision for divorce in such cases.

16. See Chapter 2, p. 35.

17. The law here differs from traditional Maliki law only in its recognition of valid excuses for separation such as business or study, a position followed by the Hanbali school.

18. While, in fact, the original intention of this law was to discourage a lighthearted or frivolous treatment of divorce and underscore the seriousness of a repudiation, hardship and injustice often occurred when an "unintended" divorce occurred as a result of a repudiation uttered under compulsion or in a state of intoxication.

19. *Article 4, Law No. 25, 1929.* However, inexplicably, formulae uttered in jest were not included.

20. See Chapter 2, p. 35.

21. Some legal scholars, such as Ibn Taymiyya, condemned *tahlil* as an abuse of the spirit of the law and thus invalid.

22. *Al-Ahram,* June 7, 1971.

23. Ibid., February 8, 1971.

24. Ibid., December 23, 1971.

25. Ibid., December 27, 1971.

26. *Law of Testamentary Dispositions, Articles 76–79, 1946.*

27. The general limitation for testamentary dispositions is one-third of the testator's estate.

28. See p. 52.

29. *Article 30, Egyptian Code of Procedure for Shari'ah Courts, 1897.*

30. *Explanatory Memorandum, Law of Rules Relevant to Waqf, 1946.*

31. However, it is noteworthy that the law did not (as it does for obligatory bequests) oblige the founder to grant the entitlement to his orphaned grandchildren.

32. Since the Indian subcontinent was a single entity prior to the partitioning of 1947 and because the legal system of Pakistan incorporated the Indian legal tradition (its laws and case history) the term India-Pakistan will be used to designate the period prior to 1947.

33. I. H. Qureshi, *The Muslim Community of the Indo-Pakistan Subcontinent (610–1947)* (The Hague: Mouton, 1961), p. 212.

34. Aziz Ahmad, *Islamic Modernism in India and Pakistan 1857–1964* (New York: Oxford University Press, 1967), p. 27.

35. As quoted in B. A. Dar, *Religious Thought of Sayyid Ahmad Khan* (Lahore: Muhammad Ashraf, 1957), p. 7.

36. Ahmad Khan, *Majmu'a Lectures* as quoted in Dar, *Religious Thought*, p. 139.

37. *Tafsir al-Qur'an*, (Lahore: 1880–1895), *al-Tahrir fi usul al-tafsir*, (Lahore: 1892), and others.

38. Ahmad, *Islamic Modernism*, pp. 74–76.

39. Chiragh Ali, *The Proposed Political, Legal and Social Reforms in the Ottoman Empire and Other Mohammedan States* (Bombay, 1883), p. 64.

40. *Ibid.*, p. 118.

41. *Ibid.*, pp. 112–13.

42. *The Egyptian Law of Inheritance of 1943* cites 270 days as its limit; see p. 136.

43. *Section 2A, Child Marriage Restraint Act, 1929.*

44. *Sections 4 and 6.* were amended by *The Muslim Family Law Ordinance, 1961, Sections 12–13,* which reduced the age of the male from twenty-one to eighteen years of age.

45. Preamble to *The Dissolution of Muslim Marriages Act, 1939.*

46. *Gazette of India* Part V (1938):36.

47. See Chapter 2, p. 17.

48. This regulation was changed to sixteen years of age by *Muslim Family Laws Ordinance of 1961.*

49. Section 2.7 of *The Dissolution of Muslim Marriages Act, 1939.*

50. See p. 57.

51. Section 2.6 of *The Dissolution of Muslim Marriages Act, 1939.* Other chronic or dangerous diseases have been included in judicial interpretations.

52. See pp. 56–57.

53. *Pakistan Legal Decision*, 1952 (W.P.) Lahore 113 (F.B.). Hereafter cited as *PLD.*

54. *PLD* 1952 (W.P.) Lahore 113 (F.B.).

55. See Chapter 2, pp. 33–34.

56. *PLD* 1959 (W.P.) Lahore 566 (paragraph 42).

57. *PLD* 1959 (W.P.) Lahore 566.

58. See p. 52.

59. Section 13 of this *Ordinance* is entitled "Amendment of the *Dissolution of Muslim Marriages Act, 1939* (VIII, 1939)" and directs that the following amendment be added to Section II regarding grounds for divorce, "(iia) that the husband has taken an additional wife in contravention of the provisions of the *Muslim Family Laws Ordinance, 1961.*"

60. See p. 56.

61. APWA *Recommendation on Family Laws Ordinance*, (Lahore: n.d.).

62. Preamble to *The West Pakistan Family Courts Act, 1964* (Act XXV of 1964).

63. Gul Newaz Khan V. Maherunnessa Begum 3 *PLD*, 1965 (E. P.) Dacca 274, 276.

64. *Report of the Commission for Eradication of Social Evils* (Government of Pakistan Ministry of Health, Labour and Social Welfare, 1965) #17.

65. Fyzee, *Outlines of Muhammadan Law*, 3rd ed., pp. 293–94.

66. *Act No. VI (Mussalman Waqf Validating Act, 1913, Section 4)*.

67. A similar defense can be found in Kemal Faruki, *Islamic Studies* 4 no. 3 (1965):264 ff.

68. The courts had taken this position repeatedly. See, for example, Aga Mahomed v. Koolson Beebe (1897), and Baker Ali Khan v. Anjuman Ara Begum (1903) 30 *India Appeals* 94.

69. Sayeeda Khanum v. Muhammad Sami (1950) *PLD* 113.

70. N. J. Coulson, *Conflicts and Tensions in Islamic Jurisprudence* (Chicago: The University of Chicago Press, 1969), pp. 106–107.

71. *Ibid.* pp. 111–12.

72. See John L. Esposito, "Pakistan: Quest for Islamic Identity" in *Islam and Development*, Ch. 8, pp. 139–62.

4—A LEGAL METHODOLOGY FOR REFORM

1. See pp. 99–101.

2. Subhi Mahmasani, *Falsafat al-Tashri fi Al-Islam*. trans. Farhat J. Ziadeh. (Leiden: E. J. Brill, 1961), p. 39.

3. Muhammad Abduh, *The Theology of Unity (Risalat* al-Tauhid) trans. Ishaq Musaad and Kenneth Cragg (London: George Allen and Unwin, 1966), p. 66.

4. *Ibid.*, pp. 39–40.

5. Muhammad Iqbal, *The Reconstruction of Religious Thought in Islam* (rpt. Lahore: Sh. Muhammad Ashraf, 1934), p. 178.

6. Ismail Ragi al-Faruqi, "Towards a New Methodology of Qur'anic Exegesis," *Islamic Studies*, (March 1962):35.

7. See, for example, *ibid.*, pp. 35–52; also S. Mahmasani, "Muslims: Decadence and Renaissance," *Muslim World* 44 (1954):192–93 and *Falsafat al-Tashri*, p. 109.

8. Al-Faruqi, "Towards a New Methodology for Qur'anic Exegesis," *Islamic Studies* (March 1962):36–37.

9. Coulson, *A History of Islamic Law*, p. 225.

10. See, for example, Ismail Ragi al-Faruqi, *On Arabism, Urubah and Religion* (Amsterdam: Djambatan, 1962), pp. 175–76; See especially Al-Faruqi's "Towards a New Methodology for Quranic Exegesis," *Islamic Studies* (March 1962):35–52 in which the need and value foundations for this approach are explored.

11. See also *Quran* III:195; IV:32; IV:124; V:41; 24:2; 28:6, et al.

12. See for example, Gustav E. von Grunebaum *Medieval Islam* (Chicago: University of Chicago Press, 1946), pp. 174–75; A. A. A. Fyzee, *A Modern Approach to Islam* (Bombay: Asia Publishing House, 1963), p. 103.

13. M. Marmaduke Pickthall, trans., *The Meaning of the Glorious Koran* (New York: Mentor, n.d.), p. 83.

14. Author's translation.

15. For a contemporary Muslim reinterpretation based upon a new grammatical and contextual analysis, see Abd al-Ati, *The Family Structure in Islam*, pp. 298 ff., especially pp. 309–16.

16. As cited in Muhammad Abdul-Rauf, *Marriage in Islam* (New York: Exposition Press, 1972), p. 14.

17. As cited in M. Mazheruddin Siddiqi, *Women In Islam* (Lahore, Pakistan: Institute of Islamic Culture, 1971), p. 60.

18. *Ibid.*, p. 80.

19. See Chapter 2, p. 20.

20. See Chapter 3, p. 51 and p. 74.

21. Mahmasani, "Muslims: Decadence and Renaissance," *Muslim World* 44 (1954):199.

22. See Chapter 1, pp. 5–7.

23. I. Goldziher, *Le dogme et al loi de l'Islam*, trans. F. Arin (Paris: Paul Geuthner, 1920); D. S. Margoliouth, *The Early Development of Mohammedanism* (London: Williams and Norgate, 1914), pp. 65–98; C. Snouch Hurgronje, *Selected Works of C. Snouch Hurgronje*, ed. C. H. Bousquet and Joseph Schacht (Leiden: Brill, 1957).

24. The significance of Schacht's views lies in the fact that he is considered by many to be the most influential Orientalist in the field of Islamic law in the twentieth century. He has deeply influenced Western scholarship through his long teaching career and his many publications on Islamic law, including the pioneering works, *Origins of Muhammadan Jurisprudence* (Oxford: Oxford University Press, 1950) and *Introduction to Islamic Law* (Oxford: Oxford University Press, 1966).

25. Joseph Schacht, *Origins of Muhammadan Jurisprudence* (Oxford: Oxford University Press, 1950), pp. 138–176.

26. Schacht, *Ibid.*, p. 140.

27. Fazlur Rahman, "Sunna and Hadith," *Islamic Studies* 1 (June 1962):4.

28. Rahman, "Concepts Sunnah, Ijtihad and Ijma in the Early Period," *Islamic Studies* 1 (1962):5.

29. Goldziher, *Muslim Studies* (London: George Allen and Unwin, 1971) 2:56.

30. Rahman, "Sunnah and Hadith," *Islamic Studies* 1 (June, 1962):13.

31. *Ibid.*, p. 31.

32. H. A. R. Gibb, *Mohammedanism* (New York: Oxford University Press, 1952), p. 86.

33. In later terminology *ray* came to mean arbitrary or personal opinion in contradistinction to the more disciplined *qiyas*.

34. Kemal Faruki, *Islamic Jurisprudence* (Karachi: Pakistan Publishing House, 1962), p. 147.

35. See, for example, *Quran* IV:29 and XVI:90.

36. See, for example, *Quran* IV:58; VII:29; and LVII:25.

37. See Chapter 1, pp. 000.

38. See, for example, Muhammah Rashid Rida, ed., *Al-Manar*, 35 vols. (Cairo: Dar al-Manar, 1898–1935), 4:858–860; and Rida, *Yusr al-Islam wa Usul al-Tashri al-Amm* (Cairo: Dar al-Manar, 1928), pp. 73 ff.

39. Chapter 3, p. 83.

40. Chapter 3, p. 66.

41. See, for example, *Quran* II:220; IV:2, 6, 10, 127; XVII:34.

42. Chapter 2, p. 39.

43. Chapter 3, p. 64.

44. *Al-Manar*, 5:181–82.

45. J. Jomier, *Le commentaire coranique du manar* (Paris: Maison-neuve, 1954), p. 193.

46. See Fazlur Rahman, *Islam* (New York: Doubleday, 1968), pp. 83–4 and Kemal Faruki, *Islamic Jurisprudence*, pp. 67 ff, and especially p. 156.

47. Ameer Ali, *The Spirit of Islam* (London: Oxford University Press, 1922), pp. 251, 278–79.

48. Iqbal, *Religious Thought in Islam*, p. 173.

49. *Ibid.*, p. 174.

50. Fazlur Rahman, "The Islamic Concept of State," in *Islam in Transition: Muslim Perspectives*, ed. John J. Donohue and John L. Esposito (New York: Oxford University Press, 1982), p. 268.

51. *Ibid.*

52. Ali Shariati "Intizar: The Religion of Protest" in Esposito, *Islam in Transition*, p. 647. See also, Rahman "The Islamic Concept of State" in Esposito, *Islam in Transition*, p. 528; Kemal Faruki, *Islamic Jurisprudence*, pp. 87, 163–64; Hassan Hanafi, "Religion and Revolution: An Islamic Model" in *Religious Dialogue and Revolution* (Cairo: The Anglo-Egyptian Bookshop, 1977), pp. 205–6.

53. Although customary practice and its Islamization may be treated within the section on *ijtihad*, for the sake of clarity, separate consideration is necessary.

54. The *Majallah* (Majallah al-Ahkam-i-Adiya) was entirely derived from Hanafi law and codified between 1869 and 1876 for use in courts of the Ottoman Empire.

55. See, for example, Abd al-Jalil Shalabi's (a former Secretary General of the Islamic Research Institute) "Personal Status Laws in Opposition with Fiqh Texts" (Qanun al-ahwal al-shakhsiyah fi muwajahat al-nusus al-fiqhiyah) in *al-Dawah*, vol. 28 (1979) 41:17–19.

56. See Cheikh Hamidou Kane, *Ambiguous Adventure* (New York: Collier Books, 1969), for a striking fictional presentation of this problem.

57. Rahman,"The Islamic Concept of State," in Esposito *Islam* (New York: Doubleday, 1968), p. 312.

58. See Mangol Bayat, "Islam in Pahlavi and Post-Pahlavi Iran: A Cultural Revolution?" in Esposito, *Islam and Development,* esp. pp. 98 ff.

59. See Fred R. von der Mehden, "Islamic Resurgence in Malaysia" in Esposito, *Islam and Development,* pp. 169–170, 173–75.

SUGGESTED READINGS

Abbot, Freeland. *Islam and Pakistan*. Ithaca, N.Y.: Cornell University Press, 1968.

Aghnides, N. P. *Mohammedan Theories of Finance*. New York: Columbia University Press, 1916.

Ahmad, Aziz. *Islamic Modernism in India and Pakistan 1857–1964*. New York: Oxford University Press, 1967.

Ahmad, K. N. *The Muslim Law of Divorce*. Islamabad: Islamic Research Institute, 1972.

Ahmad, Khurshid. *Marriage Commission Report X-Rayed*. Karachi: Charagh-i-Rah Publications, 1959.

Ali, Sayyid Ameer. *Law of Family Courts*. Karachi: Pakistan Law House, 1975.

———. *Mohammedan Law*. 6th ed. 2 Vols. Lahore: All Pakistan Legal Decisions Publ., 1965.

Anderson, J. N. D. *Islamic Law in Africa*. London: Her Majesty's Stationery Office, 1954.

———. *Islamic Law in the Modern World*. New York: New York University Press, 1959.

———. *Law Reform in the Muslim World*. London: Athlone, 1976.

Baer, Gabriel. *Population and Society in the Arab World*. London: Routledge and Kegan Paul, 1963.

Baillie, Neil B. E., trans. *A Digest of Moohummudan Law*. 4th ed. Lahore: Premier Book House, 1965.

Beck, Lois G., and Nikki Keddie, eds. *Women in the Muslim World*. Cambridge: Harvard University Press, 1978.

de Bellefonds, Y. L. *Traite de Droit Musulman Compare*. Paris: Mouton, 1965.

Berger, Morroe. *The Arab World Today*. New York: Doubleday, 1962.

Coulson, N. J. *A History of Islamic Law.* Edinburgh: Edinburgh University Press, 1964; rpt. 1978.

———. *Conflicts and Tensions in Islamic Jurisprudence.* Chicago: University of Chicago Press, 1969.

———. *Succession in the Muslim Family.* Cambridge: Cambridge University Press, 1971.

Derrett, J. D. M. *Religion, Law and the State in India.* London: The Free Press, 1968.

Donohue, John J., and John L. Esposito, eds. *Islam and Transition.* New York: Oxford University Press, 1981.

Esposito, John L., ed. *Islam and Development: Religion and Sociopolitical Change.* Syracuse: Syracuse University Press, 1980.

Al-Faruqi, Ismail Ragei. *On Arabism, Urubah and Religion.* Amsterdam: Djambatan, 1962.

Faruki, K. A. *Islamic Jurisprudence.* Karachi: Pakistan Publishing House, 1962.

Fernea, Elizabeth W., and Basima Bezirgan. *Middle Eastern Muslim Women Speak.* Austin: University of Texas Press, 1977.

Fyzee, A. A. A. *A Modern Approach to Islam.* Bombay: Asia Publishing House, 1963.

———. *Cases in the Muhammadan Law of India and Pakistan.* Oxford: Clarendon Press, 1965.

———. *Outlines of Muhammadan Law.* 4th ed. Oxford: Oxford University Press, 1974.

Gibb, H. A. R. *Mohammedanism.* New York: Oxford University Press, 1952.

Goldziher, Ignaz. *Muslim Studies.* Albany: SUNY Press, Vol. 1, 1967, Vol. 2, 1972.

Hamady, Sonia. *Temperament and Character of the Arabs.* New York: Twayne, 1960.

Hamilton, Charles, trans. *The Hedaya.* 2nd ed. Lahore: Premier Book House, 1957.

Hourani, A. H. *Arabic Thought in the Liberal Age.* Oxford: Oxford University Press, 1969.

Hurgronje, C. Snouck. *Selected Works of . . .* Edited by C. H. Bousquet and Joseph Schacht. Leiden: Brill, 1957.

Iqbal, Muhammad. *The Reconstruction of Religious Thought in Islam.* Lahore: Sh. Muhammad Ashraf, rpt. 1971.

Kerr, Malcolm. *Islamic Reform.* Berkeley: University of California Press, 1966.

Khadduri, M. *Islamic Jurisprudence.* Baltimore: Johns Hopkins University Press, 1961.

———, and H. J. Liebesny. *Law in the Middle East.* Washington, D.C.: Middle East Institute, 1955.

Khalid, Khalid M. *From Here We Start.* Trans. by Ismail R. al-Faruqi. Washington, D.C.: American Council of Learned Societies, 1953.

Levy, R. *The Social Structure of Islam.* Cambridge: Cambridge University Press, 1957.

Liebesny, H. J. *The Law of the Near and Middle East.* Albany: SUNY Press, 1975.

Macdonald, D. B. *Development of Muslim Theology, Jurisprudence and Constitutional Theory.* Lahore: Premier Book House, 1964.

Mahmasani, Subhi. *Falsafat al-Tashri fi al-Islam. (The Philosophy of Jurisprudence in Islam)* Trans. by Farhat J. Ziadeh. Leiden: Brill, 1961.

Mahmood, Shaukat. *Principles and Digest of Muslim Law.* Lahore: Pakistan Law Times Publications, 1967.

Mahmood, T. *Family Law Reform in the Muslim World.* New Delhi: N. M. Tripathi, 1972.

Maududi, A. A. *Islamic Law and Its Introduction in Pakistan.* Karachi: Charagh-i-Rah, 1955.

Merchant, M. V. *Quranic Laws.* Lahore: Sh. Muhammad Ashraf, 1947.

Mernissi, Fatima. *Beyond the Veil.* Cambridge: Schenkman, 1975.

Mulla, D. F. *Principles of Mahomedan Law.* Bombay: N. M. Tripathi, 1976.

Ostrorog, Count Leon. *The Angora Reform.* London, 1927.

Pearl, David. *A Textbook of Muslim Law.* London: Croom Helm, 1979.

Rahman, Fazlur. *Islam.* New York: Doubleday, 1968.

Ramadan, Said. *Islamic Law: Its Scope and Equity.* London: Macmillan, 1970.

Roberts, Robert. *The Social Laws of the Quran.* London: Oxford University Press, 1925.

Schacht, Joseph. *The Origins of Muhammadan Jurisprudence*. Oxford: Clarendon Press, 1950.

———. *An Introduction to Islamic Law*. Oxford: Clarendon Press, 1964.

Smith, Jane I., ed. *Women in Contemporary Muslim Societies*. Lewisburg, Pa.: Bucknell University Press, 1980.

Smith, W. Robertson. *Kinship and Marriage in Early Arabia*. Boston: Beacon Press, 1903.

Stern, Gertrude. *Marriage in Early Islam*. London: Routledge and Kegan Paul, 1939.

Tyabji, Faiz Badruddin. *Muhammadan Law: The Personal Law of Muslims*. 3rd ed. Bombay: N. M. Tripathi, 1940.

Tyan, E. *Histoire de l'organization judiciare en Pays d'Islam*. 2d ed. Leiden: Brill, 1960.

Vesey-Fitzgerald, Seymour. *Muhammadan Law: An Abridgement*. London: Oxford University Press, 1931.

von Grunebaum, G. E. *Medieval Islam*. Chicago: University of Chicago Press, 1947.

Woodsmall, Ruth F. *Women and the New East*. Washington, D.C.: Middle East Institute, 1960.

INDEX

WOMEN IN MUSLIM FAMILY LAW

was composed in 10-point VIP Caledonia and leaded 2 points,
with display type in Photo Typositor Solemnis,
by Partners Composition;
printed on 55-pound acid-free Glatfelter Antique Cream,
and adhesive bound with paper covers
by Maple-Vail Book Manufacturing Group, Inc.;
with paper covers printed in 2 colors
by Johnson City Publishing, Inc.;
and published by

Syracuse University Press
Syracuse, New York 13244-5160